Early Childhood Education

THE NATIONAL SOCIETY
FOR THE STUDY OF EDUCATION

Series on Contemporary Educational Issues
Kenneth J. Rehage, Series Editor

The 1977 Titles

Early Childhood Education: Issues and Insights, Bernard Spodek and
Herbert J. Walberg, Editors
*The Future of Big-City Schools: Desegregation Policies and Magnet
Alternatives,* Daniel U. Levine and Robert J. Havighurst, Editors
Educational Administration: The Developing Decades, Luvern L.
Cunningham, Walter G. Hack, and Raphael O. Nystrand

The National Society for the Study of Education also publishes Year-
books which are distributed by the University of Chicago Press. Inquiries regarding all publications of the Society, as well as inquiries
about membership in the Society, may be addressed to the Secretary-
Treasurer, 5835 Kimbark Avenue, Chicago, IL 60637. Membership
in the Society is open to any who are interested in promoting the investigation and discussion of educational questions.

Early Childhood Education

Issues and Insights

Edited by

BERNARD SPODEK
University of Illinois at Urbana-Champaign

HERBERT J. WALBERG
University of Illinois at Chicago Circle

McCutchan Publishing Corporation
2526 Grove Street
Berkeley, California 94704

ISBN 0-8211-1856-0

Library of Congress Catalog Card Number 76-62804

Series Foreword

The field of early childhood education has been extraordinarily active during the past decade. As the editors of this volume point out in Chapter 1, there is now a need for assessment and reflection upon the results of this activity. Because the members of the committee of the National Society for the Study of Education that is responsible for planning the series on Contemporary Educational Issues shared this view, they responded favorably to a proposal that Professors Bernard Spodek and Herbert J. Walberg compile and edit the materials contained herein.

The editors invited original contributions from several persons, all of whom have worked actively in the field of early childhood education. The objective was to provide an overview of some current issues in the field, and we believe that this volume constitutes an exceptionally useful resource for those who seek a deeper understanding of the issues.

The Society is grateful to the authors whose work made the volume possible, and especially to Professors Spodek and Walberg for their untiring efforts in planning the book and seeing it through to completion.

Other titles in the 1977 Series on Contemporary Educational Issues are:

The Future of Big-City Schools: Desegregation Policies and Magnet Alternatives, edited by Daniel U. Levine and Robert J. Havighurst; *Educational Administration: The Developing Decades,* edited by Luvern L. Cunningham, Walter G. Hack, and Raphael O. Nystrand.

Kenneth J. Rehage

for the Committee on the Expanded
Publication Program of the
National Society for the Study
of Education

Contributors

Barbara Biber, Distinguished Research Scholar, Emeritus, Bank Street College of Education

Sidney W. Bijou, Professor, Department of Special Education, University of Arizona

Vera P. John-Steiner, Professor, Department of Educational Foundations, University of New Mexico

Merle B. Karnes, Professor, Institute of Child Behavior and Development, University of Illinois at Urbana-Champaign

Lilian Katz, Professor of Early Childhood Education and Director of ERIC/ECE, University of Illinois at Urbana-Champaign

J. Ronald Lally, Director, Family Development Research Program, Syracuse University

Patricia J. Minuchin, Professor, Department of Psychoeducational Processes, Temple University

Edna Shapiro, Senior Research Associate, Research Division, Bank Street College of Education

Ellen Souberman, School of Law, University of New Mexico

Bernard Spodek, Professor of Early Childhood Education, University of Illinois at Urbana-Champaign

Herbert J. Walberg, Professor of Human Development and Learning, University of Illinois at Chicago Circle

R. Reid Zehrbach, Associate Professor, Institute for Child Behavior and Development, University of Illinois at Urbana-Champaign

Herbert Zimiles, Chairman, Research Division, Bank Street College of Education

Contents

1. Introduction:
From a Time of Plenty

Bernard Spodek and *Herbert J. Walberg*

It would appear that there is a parallel between events narrated in the Book of Genesis and the current state of research, development, and practice in the area of early childhood education. In ancient times Joseph was called upon to interpret a dream that had been troubling the Egyptian Pharaoh. Joseph's interpretation was that there would be seven years of plenty, with bountiful harvests, but that those years would be followed by seven lean years when crops would fail. Only by storing a part of the harvest during the period of abundance would Egypt survive the lean years. The dream became reality.

The mid-1960s and just beyond seemed to represent an era of plenty in the field of early childhood education. It was characterized by un-paralleled activity. Programs were provided for children not served in the past. New curriculum models were developed and evaluated. There was research relating to the characteristics of early childhood and to the impact of environmental variables on achievement and development based on naive notions concerning the power of early childhood experience and the ability of educational programs to right social wrongs. The range of goals ascribed to the programs was broader than the goals conceived earlier.

The era of abundance seems to have ended, and we face the years of scarcity. Resources that sustained earlier activities have evaporated. Service programs still in operation have been cut back by the effects of inflation. There seems to be an absence of support for the type of research and development activities that characterized the earlier period, and the optimism of that period seems also to have waned.

Just as survival in the Egypt of biblical times depended on what was stored during the time of plenty, so, perhaps, will the field of early childhood education withstand leaner times if the fruits of earlier labors are reassessed and used to achieve greater understanding and improved performance. General research and development activities may indeed no longer be possible, but assessment of programs developed earlier can continue; service programs for young children can be maintained; day-care services for children can be expanded, with new models generated; and earlier discoveries in the areas of bilingual-bicultural programs for young children and programs for young handicapped children can be utilitzed.

This waxing and waning of development activities is not new; it seems to characterize the history of early childhood education. Periodic change seems to be as much a response to changing social conditions as to the need to evaluate and assimilate the new knowledge that is rapidly generated in the field. Perhaps it is time to turn inward, to reflect upon the developments of the past decade, to assess the results of those activities, and to integrate the knowledge that has been generated into the understanding and activity of those working in the field.

It was in this same spirit of reflection, evaluation, and integration that the present volume was conceived. The chapters have been written by people who specialize in the study of early childhood education, and they are designed to begin to outline a conceptual view that allows for integration and judgment making rather than simply listing accomplishments and providing prescriptions. While each author brings unique perceptions and interests to bear on specific topics, general issues and concerns thread through the entire volume. The identification of those underlying integrative threads is also important.

During the recent productive period early childhood educators were responding to changes in the cultural context of education, changes in conceptions of learning and development, and a heightened concern for social justice. The rhetoric of the 1960s, with its references to the "war on poverty" and the civil rights movement, provides evidence of the great concern to serve all children in our nation equitably and to use educational and social programs to achieve greater equality. Schools have traditionally been an avenue of social mobility for children of the poor and of immigrant and minority groups. The idea of compensatory education was intended to make that avenue more accessible to those who had been excluded from using it successfully. Because schooling at later levels did not lead to equal access to social goods, as was traditionally expected, schooling at the early childhood level was provided as a form of compensation. Social parity was seen as the aim of programs designed for early education.

The expectations for success of programs concerned with early childhood education where educational programs at later stages had been failing resulted from changing views relating to learning and developmental theory. It was felt that efforts aimed at educating younger children might have greater long-range consequences than comparable efforts with older children. This suggestion had its greatest implications in the area of cognitive development. Emerging learning theories were also to influence new educational technologies applied to the education of young children, especially young disadvantaged children.

By evolving new social agencies, as well as involving schools in new educational activities for young children, the field was responding to changes in social needs and demands. Changes in the woman's role and in the structure of families required reevaluation of how to foster optimum development in young children. Concerns of educational institutions had to go beyond academic achievement, since achievement in early childhood is related to social and emotional development as well as to a child's health and nutritional state. Schools had to augment existing roles, generating new technologies to achieve new aims and purposes, often serving a clientele not previously served.

Patricia Minuchin's chapter on affective and social learning is based on the premise that no aspect of a child's growth progresses in isolation from other aspects. Thus the topics of affective and social learnings are viewed in a holistic framework of child development that also includes physical and cognitive development. Minuchin shows the relation of such goals of early education to Erikson's psychoanalytic theory and to Piagetian developmental concepts. She shows how these theoretical positions and goals are concretely realized in the early school environment, most notably in the curriculum and in the child's interchanges with adults and other children.

Zimiles presents contrasting views on intellectual functioning. He argues that the field of cognitive development is in disarray because the major theoretical-methodological positions — psychometrics, behaviorism, cognitive style, and cultural comparison — are incapable of integration. Early childhood educators, then, are in the difficult position of trying to optimize mental processes upon which there is little psychological consensus. The educational consequences of such shaky or conflicting psychological foundations would seem to be eclecticism, confusion, or noncomparable orthodoxies in practice.

In a complementary chapter Barbara Biber sets the theory and practice of promoting cognitive growth in young children in historical perspective. Starting with the period 1920–1940, she points to the developments in practice, some from her own work and observations, that have led to a more balanced, comprehensive understanding of the child's mental growth, one that appears to be exemplified in the Bank Street program that features enhancement of both cognitive and affective domains.

Vera John-Steiner and Ellen Souberman consider a number of issues and practices concerned with bilingual education in their chapter. They describe social developments in United States and elsewhere that have forced educators to question the role of the schools in the cause and cure of cultural conflict and to discuss the principal issues bearing upon bilingual education and early childhood: the population requiring such education, models of bilingual teaching and learning, the cultural dimensions of bilingual education, and the role of evaluation.

Ronald Lally brings a decade of experience in infant education and contemporary theory and research to bear upon misunderstandings concerning development, the influence of parent and child on one another, the infant's tastes, and the role of the environment. He finds a consensus emerging among educators of infants concerning high-quality care and guidelines for infant education.

Merle Karnes and Reid Zehrbach, after noting the contributions of several pioneers in early education for the handicapped, develop three classifications that capture the principal ways that contemporary programs vary: program characteristics, contexts, and instructional models. The authors cite a number of centers in the United States that illustrate the program features described, and they conclude their chapter with an analysis of the components of an exemplary program.

Bernard Spodek reviews program conceptions in early childhood education, identifying a concern for the support of development and a concern for the achievement of specific learnings that have characterized alternative curriculum conceptions throughout the history of early childhood education and continue to characterize them today. A number of ways of analyzing educational programs for young children are discussed, and some comparative studies of program outcomes are reviewed.

After citing the major originators and contemporary exemplars of behavior analysis in early childhood education, Sydney Bijou adopts a behavioral point of view in discussing the philosophy or goals of teaching, teaching methods available to achieve expressed goals, and the supports required by the teacher to attain those goals. Under each topic, Bijou traces the implications of behavioral research for understanding and improving early education.

Edna Shapiro argues that evaluation can distort and hamper programs concerned with early education. Funding agencies, for example, often require unrealistic promises from proposal writers, and evaluators may debase teaching by reducing its qualities to minute, trivial acts and its results to isolated psychometric items on standardized achievement tests. Although parents, teachers, and children may be well satisfied with a program, evaluation instruments and designs may be too narrow or insensitive to detect its accomplishments. Shapiro cites a number of ways to strengthen evaluation and make it more useful to policy makers.

In the final chapter Lilian Katz draws on the sociological concept of "professional socialization" to analyze teacher education. For her, eight factors bear heavily upon the socialization of students preparing to teach in early education programs, and they are the goals of the program, the characteristics of the candidates, the characteristics of the staff, the content, the timing of the educational activities, the ethos or intellectual spirit of the program, the location and setting, and regulatory agencies. She concludes that, in contrast to the extensive research available on the effects of teaching, far less is known about the effect of socializing agents on the teacher.

These, then, are the topics covered. This book is not a complete review of the state of the art of early childhood education; nor is it encyclopedic in its coverage. Rather, it represents an attempt to identify issues in selected aspects of the field, present major concerns, and analyze selected aspects of knowledge pertaining to early childhood education. The topics treated were selected not only because they represent issues within the field of early childhood education but also because they represent areas in which present knowledge could be reviewed and conceptualized. To some extent any selection also represents the tastes and interests of the editors. Among the many issues that could be only briefly discussed, the following deserve special mention:

Delivery systems for early childhood education. Many issues can be identified in the field today relating to the nature of institutions that could best serve young children. The use of public schools to deliver educational and social services to young children is advocated by a number of groups made up primarily of public school teachers. This suggestion is being challenged by those involved in the private sector of early childhood education: operators of nursery schools and day-care centers that provide services on a tuition or fee basis. In addition to public schools and individual entrepreneurial early childhood centers, a number of chain and franchise operations have developed to provide services to young children. Comprehensive community-based consortia have also evolved to serve young children and their families. It would be important not only to identify the issues involved in the debate about which arrangement best serves young children, but also to consider what has been learned from each of the delivery systems.

Day care reconceptualized. A generation ago, day care was considered a service for poor children and their families, while the more affluent sent their children to nursery schools. With an increase in the number of working mothers and single-parent families, as well as increasing demands for equity among women in current society, there has been a greater demand for day-care service and a change in the conception of day-care and its clientele. Day care now provides a range of services for a variety of people, and it has encountered both strong support and strong opposition. In this area, too, an identification of issues and a marshalling of information in regard to the service and its consequences for children and parents would render an important service in the field.

The role of parents in early childhood education. During the early part of this century parents were regarded essentially as secondary clients in programs for young children. As a result of both the cooperative nursery school movement and the parent participation requirements of Head Start programs, parents have been seen more as policy makers than as persons to be educated. With increased concern for parents' rights, teachers' rights, and children's rights, the venerable notion that all parties involved in the education of young children are essentially concerned with doing what is best for the young child is being questioned. Indeed, there may be no agreement as to what is considered best for the child. Each person involved in the complex relationships connected with early childhood programs might have a distinct set of interests that conflict with the interests of others. We need to look again at the role of parents in early childhood programs and at the many possible relations that can and do exist between parent and teacher.

There are other issues equally worthy of study and analysis. Any one book can only help to illuminate a portion of the complex and panoramic field of early childhood education. It is our hope and expectation that this book will provide some illumination or at least help to identify the confusion that exists. If it cannot resolve that confusion, it can at least help the reader understand some of the issues and ideas related to several specific topics.

2. Affective and Social Learning in the Early School Environment

Patricia Minuchin

In order to talk about affective and social learning, it is first necessary to establish the basic premise that no aspect of development moves along in isolation. A child's relationships, feelings, and adaptations to social context are bound to each other and to "cognitive" efforts to explore, create, and make sense of the world. None of these takes precedence or is more basic; all are simultaneous and interacting processes, and all are shaped by the early educational environment. If one accepts this premise, it is possible to consider those aspects of early development most concerned with relationships and feelings and with the ways in which a young child's experience in school affects the perception of others, the concept of self, and the expression and management of feelings.

INTERPERSONAL AND AFFECTIVE GOALS FOR YOUNG CHILDREN

Goals for young children's development are implicitly related to images of the fulfilled and productive adult. Such images set general criteria for healthy development compatible with the Western view of what makes life worth living. Attempts to define the healthy personality repeatedly refer to the ability to establish meaningful relationships,

8

to be resilient and flexible, to express feelings and channel expression in ways both satisfying to the individual and reasonably acceptable to others, to develop a differentiated self-concept that allows acceptance of foibles and appreciation of strength, and to the capacity for investing oneself in terms of experience, productive effort, and the social context.[1]

For young children the goals are more modest, but they express the same themes. They deal with early forms of exploration and mastery in relating to other people and in handling stimulation from inside as well as outside the self, and they deal both with the enhancement of pleasure and with the development of viable forms of control. Some of the goals may be listed as:

— the expansion of trusting relationships to adults beyond the family and to peers;
— the increasing development of channels for expressing and managing fear, helplessness, anger, affection, and excitement;
— the establishment of foundations for cooperative interaction in work and play;
— the maintenance of an exploratory stance toward the environment and of a capacity for choice and initiative;
— the enhancement of a subjective sense of mastery and of the power to communicate and to make an impact on the environment.[2]

Like the family, the early school environment has vast potential for furthering such goals and learning. What happens to the child, however, is a complex function of the experiences that are offered and of the child's own capacities and propensities for making use of them. The nature of what is offered defines the boundaries of potential growth. Within those boundaries the child selects, explores, and reconstructs in keeping with the issues that have the most meaning and which fit the child's own potential for understanding, expression, and control. For those who design and implement early environments, it is important to know what the child brings into school, both as an individual and as a person in relatively early stages of development.

PRESCHOOL DEVELOPMENT: CHARACTERISTICS AND LIMITATIONS

Much is known about the characteristics and limitations of young children. Developmental theory, research, and careful observation suggest that there are salient psychological issues to be worked through, that there are characteristic modes of grasping experience, and that there are particular avenues through which young children express and explore what they feel and what they are learning.

Salient Psychological Issues

Erik Erikson has provided a theoretical framework for understanding the psychological issues that have primacy as people move through the different stages of their life cycle.[3] Young children, in his view, deal psychologically with the dependability of other people and with the effects of their own efforts to explore and create an impact. He calls these the issues of trust, autonomy, and initiative. These psychological issues are implicitly worked and reworked in all encounters between the child and the environment. The sense of trust, confidence, and self-worth that shapes slowly through such experiences depends primarily on the way in which other people react to the child's needs and efforts.

A vast psychological literature explores the processes of attachment and separation in very young children and points to the same issues.[4] The child's strong attachment to a primary adult figure is seen as crucial for forging a link to the world and other people, but it is equally important that the child venture out and explore, extending confidence to others and gaining the self-confidence needed to act autonomously. Such processes, fraught with strong feelings of both pleasure and anxiety, are worked through first in the family context and during the earliest years, but the young child who goes to school reworks them in a new context and with new people: Who can be trusted and depended on? If one ventures forth to explore in this environment and runs into trouble, will anyone comfort and resolve the difficulties? What feelings can be expressed and accepted? What happens if one breaks something or is afraid? How does one play with others, asserting one's own preferences and safety and sharing or adapting without loss of personal investment? The child brings a set of expectations into the new setting, but it is necessary to test and revise, constantly learning new things about people, about the rules of interchange, and about the self. The balance among dependence, autonomy, and interdependence with others remains a lifelong issue, but it is psychologically crucial in a child's early years. The school setting is a natural workshop for expanding the knowledge of patterns and possibilities learned first within the family.

The Egocentric Orientation toward the World

Characteristic modes of thought, at this young level, determine what young children perceive and can learn through their experiences. Jean Piaget has taught us much about the egocentric orientation of the preschool child—the unquestioned assumption that others share his or her experience and perspective and that all events are related to the self.[5] The most familiar illustrations, perhaps, are concrete and perceptual, for example, a four-year-old describes a pattern accurately, on request, as he or she perceives it. When asked how it looks to another person sitting opposite, the child describes it in exactly the same way. There are parallel examples for social and affective interchange, and the same limitations are evident. The child communicates with others from within a personal framework and interprets the actions and feelings of other people as they impinge on the self. The capacity to empathize with feelings and intentions, understand another's viewpoint, or communicate so that meaning is clear requires, in its more organized forms, that one be able to shift perspective, understand that different perspectives exist, and hold one's own viewpoint and that of the other person in mind at the same time. Developmental studies have shown that such capacities depend upon a general reorganization of thought toward concrete-operational processes and nonegocentric perspectives, and they do not become firmly established until the middle years.[6] Young children can be taught socialized responses—to apologize, to wait, to share—but such responses do not indicate, nor necessarily even hasten, the development of a truly social perspective. The young child lacks the developmental characteristics that would allow understanding of or empathy with another person's situation and enable the child to relate and communicate accordingly.

This is not to say that such capacities are completely absent through early childhood. They are in a formative stage. Any parent or teacher has seen young children concerned with the distress of another person, and psychologists have recently probed the young forms of empathy, role taking, and helping behavior that tend to appear in simple, familiar, and emotionally meaningful situations.[7] One psychologist has described the changing forms of empathy during the early years within a theoretical framework. The very youngest children, he notes, have no clear sense of a separate self or of other people as independent entities; they may, however, show "simple empathic distress," in response to perceptions of other people's pain. Once the separation between the self and others is clear, a "sympathetic" response becomes possible, based on the understanding that it is somebody *else* who is in distress. It must be recognized that, in the simplest form of such reactions, both the problem and its resolution are conceptualized in terms that are egocentric and would fit the self. Somewhat later in the preschool period, with increasing maturity and relevant experience, the child may make more effort to understand what is happening to the other person, though complex shifts in perspective, as noted earlier, come still later,[8] and the nature of the child's experience is crucial to this development.

It is the growth of new cognitive structures that creates new potential for understanding others, for sympathetic concern, and for reciprocal relationships. Such developments do not inevitably occur. The child learns in accord with the kinds of experience offered in the family and in other major environments such as school.

Characteristic Modes of Exploration and Expression

There are other characteristics of young children important to consider in constructing a growth-supporting school environment. *Action* and *movement* are characteristic vehicles for discharging energy, processing information, and feeling effective. *Language* grows in importance as a means of communication and as an alternative to action in communicating with others and in resolving conflict. And *play* serves as the crucial medium through which the child expresses feelings, explores roles and relationships, creates a domain of personal control, and consolidates the meaning of experience. Action, language, and play are natural media for all young children.

In spite of the many differences among individual children, all enter school with some common characteristics that define early stages in the life cycle. They have psychological concerns that are developmentally relevant and thus predictable, they make sense of the world through the egocentric patterns of thought that are available to them, and they explore and master experience through modes that are playful and action oriented. Such characteristics shape the child's selection, processing, and learning in any area of development, and the educator who would advance the child toward positive goals must recognize them and work with them.

THE EARLY SCHOOL ENVIRONMENT

How do children learn in the school environment? What are the experiences that affect their perceptions and relations with others, their knowledge of themselves, and the emotional tone of their contacts and self-perceptions? Much of what is learned depends on interchange with other children and on experience with adults, but other aspects of school, such as the structure and content of the curriculum, have a less obvious, less direct effect.

Curriculum and Classroom Structure

Ongoing experience with materials and learning is usually thought of as cognitive. From such experience, however, the child realizes general as well as specific learning—matters of attitude and orientation—and these apply to social situations and to self-understanding, as well as to learning in the subject area. In good classrooms for young children, for instance, teachers often work with materials and activities that sensitize children to the world around them, educating their capacities to observe, to notice similarities in disparate objects, and to differentiate qualities and details. Formal materials created for the Montessori schools many years ago stressed the different feel of textures and gradations of sounds, size, and weight. In more informal, gamelike ways, teachers often have children shut their eyes and listen to various sounds or try to identify the contents of a bag by its smell and feel. It is perhaps the best of teachers who builds alertness and noticing into all activities—a discussion of gerbils in the classroom, a walk to observe different styles of houses on the school block, and so on. Such an orientation toward observing and differentiating is ultimately helpful in learning to read or in thinking through a problem, but it also stimulates the awareness of subtle cues from other people about their needs and moods. It may also heighten alertness to the inner experience of tension or buried anger, or affect the perception of the environment as changing and interesting rather than vague and boring. Any experience registers at several levels, and a child, unfettered by the label "concept formation time," integrates and applies the learning wherever it is useful. If schemata are formed for noticing and differentiating stimuli, then they are available to the child in any sphere and any encounter. What is important is that the experiences for forming such schemata be made available in a variety of contexts.

Other curriculum activities have this same multilevel meaning. One practical effect of Piaget's ideas about preoperational thought and about the importance of direct experience for fostering conceptual growth has been that an increasing number of educators have developed environments and curricula meant to foster such developments.[9] In some instances they promote direct experience with conservation or other activities to lessen egocentric tendencies. In other instances they provide a wide variety of materials to manipulate and explore, assigning the child a generally active and participatory role. In either instance it is assumed that the child's activities and the feedback from interaction will advance the capacity to understand connections between parts of a process and hold several qualities in mind at once, and go beyond the self. Again, the experiences that support greater mental flexibility and perspective serve to increase the potential for perceiving other points of view or for understanding that I, myself, may seem different to others than I do to myself.

The many kinds of communication that are part of the learning interchange also pertain to a child's social development and the management of feelings. What is crucial here, perhaps, is the teacher's attitude toward the child's efforts and contributions. Most programs for young children, especially those directed toward compensatory early education for the disadvantaged, have stressed the development of language skills.[10] They have emphasized the labeling of objects, the rehearsal of names of concepts, the accuracy of pre-positions, and similar activities. These are obviously important. Some educators have, however, viewed language in different terms. They have seen the child's deficiency, in many cases, as being absence of trust, inability or unwillingness to communicate, and lack of confidence in oneself, as well as specific language inadequacies.[11] From this point of view the helpful emphasis is on making contact, on accepting nonverbal communication even though words might be encouraged, and on attentive listening while children grope for the words needed to express an idea. Such an attitude is relevant at any socioeconomic level. Even articulate children grope for words when they have a half-formed insight, are struggling with a new connection, or are trying to communicate a personal experience that is associated with something that is new. The teacher who waits and encourages communication conveys a respect for integrative ideas, for personalized learning, and for the worth of the child. Experience in communicating an idea and having it received certainly affects self-esteem. It also increases trust in the viability of language as a means of resolving such difficult or personal situations as arguing with another child or confiding to a teacher something that is frightening or considered shameful.

Other activities and structures that define the program and fill the school day have similar direct or indirect effects. It matters whether the room and the schedule are organized for freedom of movement and choice; whether there is space and equipment for vigorous, large-muscle activities; whether there is opportunity for dramatic play; and whether there is a mixture of time with oneself, time with another child or two, and time with the whole group when, guided by the teacher, the group can function as a small society, resolving the issues of group life as they arise. Such activities and structures relate to goals described earlier. They relate, for instance, to the sense the one guides one's own life a bit, even in a world of powerful grown-ups, through exercising choice and through controlling the domain of play. They relate to a sense of effectiveness and an awareness of one's power and limitations in a variety of contexts. And they relate to the grasp of human interaction through reliving experience in dramatic play, as well as through direct participation in the different levels of contact inherent in small and large groups. Early school environments provide the first paradigm outside the family of how a society functions, with its rules, structures, and pathways of communication. The capacity to grasp or articulate the workings of such a society does not come until middle childhood. Early experiences do, however, lay a foundation for later understanding, and the nature of the preschool classroom affects the way that the child accumulates learning about social organization, the nature of authority, and the possibilities for individual freedom and effectiveness within an organized social context.

Interchange with Peers

Interacting with other children is, of course, a proving ground for social learning. In this, the early school environment is a natural and major context for growth. Most preschool programs and "open" elementary classrooms provide opportunity for spontaneous contact, for working and playing together, and for forming and dissolving friendships, with all the tribulations and pleasures that accompany such experiences.

Here it becomes more difficult to talk generally about "the young child" and his or her use of such opportunities. Children change great-ly between the ages of two and six in their spontaneous contacts with other children, and their social reactions vary further by subgroup and by individual. Systematic studies show what might have been predic-ted through careful observation: between two and six years of age children increasingly seek the company of other children and turn less automatically to adults. A turning point may come somewhere around the age of four when children play together more, giving, attending, responding, arguing, and generally interacting.[12] The earliest forms of contact involve parallel play—companionably near another child but not playing together. As the child gradually comes to interact more with other children, again at about the age of four, such activities as cooperative block building and varieties of shared dramatic play occur more frequently in the classroom.

These contacts offer the richest kind of experience for learning about friendship, communication, other people's opinions, and the kind of behavior acceptable to other children. Through such contacts children express their own ideas and needs, and they observe and imi-tate each other. Researchers find that preschool children copy both the aggression and the helpfulness they see in others.[13] In one study even the fearful behavior of children with dog phobias was modified by observing other children who were not afraid.[14]

Some children are more gregarious than others and easily reap the benefits of social contact. In contrast, it may require freedom of move-ment in a classroom for quiet and less outgoing children to find com-fortable groups or a compatible friend. In an observational study of six-year-olds in open classrooms, for instance, Minuchin's sample in-cluded two children who were constantly together through the year-long period of observation.[15] They had each been chosen for study, along with others, as children with cautious and reserved styles of ap-proaching the environment and, indeed, they were not particularly active in reaching out to others. Their experience in school, however, was one of constant interaction, exchanging information, asking and giving help, working together, and generally developing toward social patterns that were adaptive and satisfying. For these children, social learning was worked out in intensive experience with one other child rather than extensive experience with many other children. Such ex-periences differ in style, but they do not necessarily differ in value.

Although the ultimate goal is "cooperative interaction in work and play," only the foundations of cooperation can be laid in early child-hood, even among good friends in supportive climates guided by help-ful and sensitive teachers. Research on cooperative behavior suggests that people are most likely to help and share when their goals are in-terdependent and when cooperation holds some benefit for the self.[16] Perhaps this requires not only a direct perception of benefit but also a capacity to understand the relation between immediate behavior and ultimate results, as well as a capacity to delay gratification. It may also involve some sense of identification with a group purpose, so that the individual does not need to receive a tangible and individual benefit. None of these capacities is well established in early childhood, either emotionally or intellectually. The child does not begin to identify strongly with peer group purposes until the middle years, and, as has been noted earlier, the organized grasp of how specific behavior fits into larger patterns is not part of a preoperational, egocentric orienta-tion to the world. In a relevant study of cooperation in four-year-olds, the patterns that emerged were interesting and predictable.[17] The children could work together when there were rewards for both, but, when only one prize was offered, one child usually dominated or they were so competitive that they did not qualify for a prize at all. Chil-dren so young are unable to see the ultimate benefit of taking turns and helping each other under competitive pressures. The require-ments of an organized strategy are too complex; children are primar-ily aware of the immediate loss of benefits.

If these are the developmental realities, cooperative behavior can-not be forced in a preschool setting. It is possible, however, to provide ample opportunity for playing and working together, so that the ex-perience of shared mastery and of the possibilities for resolving con-flict can slowly build a foundation for later and more sustained mutu-ality. Young children should have both easy access to and easy exit from such situations, and adults must be ready to mediate difficulties, when necessary, so that children do not move toward destructive solu-tions and learnings.

The expression and management of aggression is, of course, a cen-tral issue in children's interaction. Whenever there is vigorous play, movement, and materials to be shared, clashes of purpose and feeling are inevitable. Jane and Clara both want the paintbrush; Harold steps on Amy's hand in his dash across the room; Rhonda hurts Arlo's feel-ings. Reactions to such events change in form during the early years.

Hitting, pushing, and sometimes even biting are common in the youngest children. As they gain firmer control of the language, physical aggression decreases, and verbal expressions of insult and complaint increase. Open aggression as a whole declines as children grow older.[18]

In early childhood, at least, the idea that some children are aggressive while others are pleasant and helpful is not particularly valid. On closer inspection some of the same children who express aggression are found to be helpful and to make positive contact as well.[19] For these children an underlying vigor and assertiveness may govern active contact with others, their attitude of give and take, and spontaneous expressions of feeling, whether affectionate or angry. Anger needs to be channeled, but not extinguished or suppressed. Psychodynamic theory maintains that anger is an inevitable part of the self and that it is best accepted as such without denial or excessive shame. The task of socialization is to direct such feelings into forms of expression that will not be destructive. For preschool children this means the channeling of temper into words rather than blows, using language both to discharge feeling and to seek some resolution.

Often such situations require a teacher's intervention. This need not be automatic or early, however, since the experience of conflict and children's attempts to resolve it themselves are important parts of growth. In his discussion of how language and thought mature, Piaget argues that quarreling performs a constructive function by assisting in "reflection" and helping to develop a socialized perspective.[20] For the young child, disagreements with another child provide concrete evidence that one's egocentric needs are not self-evident. One child comes to perceive that another child has a different opinion. Then the child must justify, or demonstrate, or explain his or her own need ("I have to have it for my building—right there."). Quarrels need to run their course, based on this point of view, since they spur the development of multiple perspectives and demonstrate the need to communicate clearly, in a context where motivation is high. Preschool children cannot really exchange views in a logical, systematic way, according to Piaget. His investigations showed that true argument based on shared conceptions appeared only in the early elementary years. During the earlier period, however, children do move through preparatory stages—from action to the simple clash of contrary opinions to primitive attempts to justify—and such experience is necessary and valuable. For the teaching adult, of course, the total context is important in deciding whether to intervene. When arguments frustrate children or accelerate to fights, the children may learn little from their own efforts, and the degree of emotion may be upsetting. At such moments, the teacher's mediation may provide the paradigm for explanation and an exchange of views ("What did you want Barry to do, Marcia?" "How did you feel about that?"), as well as a sense that conflict can be accepted and alternative solutions found.

The Role of Adults

Adults are crucial to the child's social learning in childhood. In the school setting it is the teacher who selects and guides the learning experience. The teacher scans what is happening between children and decides whether to intervene. The teacher also becomes a central figure for the child, teaching many things about relationships and feelings by example and contact.

In psychological theory, two principles are always invoked to explain the processes by which children learn social behavior from the adult: direct socialization or teaching, and "identification" or "modeling." Psychodynamic, behavioristic, and social learning theories tend to use their own terms for these principles, and perhaps all theories are more formal and detached than parents or teachers tend to be. There would, however, probably be general agreement about some basic ideas. We are all quite sure that children learn social patterns from adults by observing how adults live as people. Children also learn through the impact of direct contact, which teaches the child what to do through indications of adult satisfaction with or disapproval of a child's spontaneous reactions. From such observations and interactions children learn at two levels. They come to understand what behavior is acceptable, and they form basic attitudes toward themselves and others. Their conception of self, their acceptance of impulse, their trust, and their adaptation to authority are all strongly affected by those adults who are important in their lives.

It is the family that provides the first context for such learning, but the teacher expands the child's image of how authority is carried, how affect is expressed, and how people care for others. In theoretical terms, we can talk of teachers as potential models for "prosocial behavior" and for the expression of a differentiated range of affect. In experiential terms, a child is influenced in similar directions by a teacher who shares an apple with a group of children, who washes a scraped knee gently so it will not hurt, who helps with a learning problem, who protects a scapegoat, who explains why a rule makes sense, or who expresses a wide range of feelings in the course of daily interaction. A host of experimental studies have tested children's responses to adult modeling of one kind of behavior or another, such as nurturance, aggression, or "yielding to temptation," and the power of adult example is almost unnerving in such studies.[21] What is almost certainly true is that children try out many things, sifting and discarding as they go, and that adults prominent in the child's life have the greatest influence. Children identify most strongly with adults who are nurturant and close and who have sustained power over the child's life. It is the behavior and style of these people, often adult members of the family and well-loved teachers whose patterns are observed most closely, imitated, transformed into personal, childlike forms, and integrated into the child's own repertoire.

The child's particular relationship to the teacher mediates his or her learning most directly. It is through individual contacts that the child learns what is acceptable or not acceptable and reworks the salient psychological issues of the early childhood years. Teachers are sometimes described as "substitute mothers," especially for the youngest preschool children, but it is possibly because they are *not* mother that good teachers contribute most to a child's growth. A different individual in a different context, who also cares for the child, responds to need, and encourages autonomous exploration, expands the child's world. The child relates to a new person who has a different style and pace, and it is through such contacts that differentiated schemata of trust, autonomy, and initiative are developed. The teacher's role in this reworking of basic issues is complex. Optimally, it is idiosyncratic for each child. Andy needs basically to be accepted and appreciated; Sybil is ready for new experiences, but the teacher must go with her for a bit each time before she can move on her own; Dawn tests boundaries provocatively, while Graham is unaware he has crossed them. The sensitive teacher relates differently to each, though the basic ingredients of support, control, and encouragement toward mastery and growth are constant.

Out of these individualized relationships, the child learns much about the self. Some theorists see the sense of self and self-worth as growing from the "reflected appraisals" of people important to the child.[22] The teacher's understanding and appraisal, communicated in an individualized way, helps the child form a conception of self — a process in early and amorphous development during the preschool years — and a sense of whether he or she is valued and lovable. Affectionate hugs and generalized praise are probably not enough for optimal growth. A teacher needs to know the children well enough to react to the characteristic patterns and the frontiers of mastery of each child ("That's a different kind of house you're painting today, Benjy").

The teacher's reaction to impulse expression is particularly important for the child's developing attitude toward the self. As children learn that some feelings must be controlled or diverted, the possibilities increase that they will feel excessive guilt about angry outbursts or destructive fantasies and that their feelings will be buried, denied, or go unrecognized. The adult task is subtle: to help keep such feelings conscious and available, while helping children to control and channel expression. In order to encourage free communication of feeling and personal association in the classroom, some gamelike techniques have recently been developed for use with classroom groups.[23] They make use of such procedures as sitting in a "magic circle," role playing, and discussing individual experiences and feelings, often on prescribed topics ("Something I do very well is . . . "; "I made someone feel bad when I . . . "), with certain rules about not interrupting and about accepting each other's contributions.[24] Some teachers find such procedures useful, even with young children, for validating personal experience and exploring conflict, pleasure, anxiety, and concern for others in an open way. These are interesting ways of teaching social and emotional attitudes, but they are essentially supplementary. Children do not learn basic attitudes from direct affective curricula. They learn predominantly from immediate, continuous experiences with people, materials, and their own impulses, and it is the quality of teacher mediation and guidance during moments marked by strong emotion that have the greatest impact on the direction of learning.

Most of this chapter has been cast in positive terms, emphasizing developmental goals for children and referring to experiences and relationships that might advance those goals. Children learn something about social relationships, authority, the acceptability of impulse, and their own worth in any kind of classroom, however. If a teacher screams "Don't raise your voice to me!" the children learn that the world is confusing. If the curriculum is narrow and pedantic, their horizons are not expanded. If they are ridiculed, ignored, and frequently scolded, they learn to withhold trust and to devalue themselves. If control is stressed and motivation or feeling is disqualified, they learn to dissociate behavior from inner experience. The issue is not *whether* relationships, self-image, and style of expression will be affected by the early school environment. It is, rather, *how* such developments will be affected. Each child brings a very personal image of self, other people, and the world into the classroom and assimilates and adapts to experiences in his or her own way. That environment and the people in it will certainly affect the general quality of growth in all of the children. The educational task is to shape learning toward forms of personal development and human interchange that might improve the quality of life for the individual and for society.

Notes

1. Marie Jahoda, *Current Concepts of Positive Mental Health* (New York: Basic Books, 1958).
2. See also Scarvia Anderson and Samuel Messick, *Social Competency in Young Children* (Princeton, N.J.: Educational Testing Service, 1973); Barbara Biber, "A Learning-Teaching Paradigm Integrating Intellectual and Affective Processes," in *Behavioral Science Frontiers in Education*, ed. Eli M. Bower and William G. Hollister (New York: John Wiley & Sons, 1967), 111–155; Edna Shapiro and Barbara Biber, "The Education of Young Children: A Developmental-Interaction Approach," *Teachers College Record* 74 (September 1972): 55–79.
3. Erik Erikson, *Childhood and Society* (New York: W. W. Norton & Co., 1950).
4. Mary D. Salter Ainsworth and Barbara A. Wittig, "Attachment and Exploratory Behavior of One-Year-Olds in a Strange Situation," in *Determinants of Infant Behavior IV*, ed. Brian M. Foss (New York: John Wiley & Sons, 1967), 111–136; John Bowlby, *Attachment and Loss* (New York: Basic Books, 1969); Eleanor E. Maccoby and John C. Masters, "Attachment and Dependency," in *Carmichael's Manual of Child Psychology*, 2 vols., ed. Paul H. Mussen (New York: John Wiley & Sons, 1970), 2:73–157.
5. Jean Piaget, *The Construction of Reality in the Child* (New York: Basic Books, 1954); *id., Six Psychological Studies* (New York: Random House, 1967).
6. Dorothy Flapan, *Children's Understanding of Social Interaction* (New York: Teachers College Press, 1968); John Flavell *et al., The Development of Role-Taking and Communication Skills in Children* (New York: John Wiley & Sons, 1968).
7. Helene Borke, "Interpersonal Perception of Young Children: Egocentrism or Empathy?" *Developmental Psychology* 5 (September 1971): 263–269; Kathryn A. Urberg and Edward M. Docherty, "The Development of Role-Taking Skills in Young Children," paper presented at meetings of the Society for Research in Child Development, Denver, 1975; Marian R. Yarrow and Carolyn Z. Waxler, "The Emergence and Functions of Prosocial Behaviors in Young Children," paper presented at meetings of the Society for Research in Child Development, Denver, 1975.

8. Martin L. Hoffman, "Developmental Synthesis of Affect and Cognition and Its Implications for Altruistic Motivation," *Developmental Psychology* 11 (September 1975): 607-622.

9. Constance Kamii, "A Sketch of the Piaget-Derived Pre-school Curriculum Developed by the Ypsilanti Early Education Program," in *History and Theory of Early Childhood Education*, ed. Samuel J. Braun and Esther P. Edwards (Worthington, Ohio: Charles A. Jones Publishing Co., 1972), 295-312; Celia Stendler Lavatelli, "A Piaget-Derived Model for Compensatory Pre-school Education," in *Early Childhood Education Rediscovered*, ed. Joe L. Frost (New York: Holt, Rinehart and Winston, 1968), 530-544; *Piaget in the Classroom*, ed. Milton Schwebel and Jane B. Raph (New York: Basic Books, 1973).

10. Eleanor E. Maccoby and Miriam Zellner, *Experiments in Primary Education: Aspects of Project Follow-Through* (New York: Harcourt Brace Jovanovich, 1970).

11. Barbara Biber, "Goals and Methods in a Preschool Program for Disadvantaged Children," *Children* 17 (January-February 1970): 15-20; Patricia Minuchin and Barbara Biber, "A Child Development Approach to Language in the Preschool Disadvantaged Child," Monograph No. 124, in *Language Remediation for the Disadvantaged Preschool Child*, ed. Marvin A. Brottman, *Monographs of the Society for Research in Child Development* 33 (No. 8, 1968): 10-18.

12. Rosalind Charlesworth and Willard W. Hartup, "Positive Social Reinforcement in the Nursery School Peer Group," *Child Development* 38 (December 1967): 993-1002; Dina Feitelson, Shoshana Weintraub, and Ora Michaeli, "Social Interactions in Heterogeneous Preschools in Israel," *ibid.*, 43 (December 1972): 1249-1259; Willard W. Hartup, "Peer Interaction and Social Organization," in *Carmichael's Manual of Child Psychology* 2:361-456.

13. Hartup, "Peer Interaction and Social Organization."

14. Albert Bandura, Joan E. Grusec, and Frances L. Menlove, "Vicarious Extinction of Avoidance Behavior," *Journal of Personality and Social Psychology* 5 (January 1967): 16-23.

15. Patricia Minuchin, "Differential Use of the Open Classroom: A Study of More and Less Exploratory Children," National Institute of Education Grant #NL-G-00-3-0018, 1973. ERIC: ED 103 117.

16. Morton Deutsch, "An Experimental Study of the Effects of Co-operation and Competition upon Group Process," *Human Relations* 2 (July 1949): 199-231.

17. Millard Madsen and Linden Nelsen, "Cooperation and Competition in Four-Year-Olds as a Function of Reward Contingency and Subculture" (1968), cited in Edith Grotberg, *Review of Research 1965-1969* (Washington, D.C.: Project Head Start, Office of Economic Opportunity, U.S. Department of Health, Education, and Welfare, 1969), 15.

18. Hartup, "Peer Interaction and Social Organization."

19. Lynn Dorman, "The Expression of Aggression in Pre-school Children," 1967 (PS 001 255), cited in Grotberg, *Review of Research 1965-1969*, 14; Yarrow and Waxler, "Emergence and Functions of Prosocial Behaviors."

20. Jean Piaget, *The Language and Thought of the Child* (New York: Harcourt, Brace, 1926).

21. Albert Bandura, Dorothea Ross, and Sheila A. Ross, "Transmission of Aggres-

sion through Imitation of Aggressive Models," *Journal of Abnormal and Social Psychology* 63 (November 1961): 575-582; Aletha Huston Stein, "Imitation of Resistance to Temptation," *Child Development* 38 (March 1967): 157-169; Marian R. Yarrow and Phyllis M. Scott, "Imitation of Nurturant and Nonnurturant Models," *Journal of Personality and Social Psychology* 23 (August 1974): 259-270.

22. Harry Stack Sullivan, *The Interpersonal Theory of Psychiatry* (New York: W. W. Norton & Co., 1953).

23. Harold Bessell and Uvaldo Palomares, *Methods in Human Development*, Lesson Guide, Level B (San Diego, Calif.: Human Development Training Institute, 1969); Gloria Castillo, *Left-Handed Teaching: Lessons in Affective Education* (New York: Praeger Publishers, 1975).

24. Bessell and Palomares, *Methods in Human Development.*

3. Contrasting Views of Intellectual Functioning and Their Implications for Education

Herbert Zimiles

The question of how the intellect functions and how this can most accurately be measured presents a paradox. The very idea of intellectual development is almost universally graspable and therefore usually taken for granted. Each person has experienced his own intellectual growth, has observed it in a multitude of forms among others, and has attended institutions expressly concerned with fostering intellectual development. Hardly any psychological concept seems to be more real. At the same time, it remains agonizingly nebulous and ill defined. Despite almost a century of research, psychologists cannot agree upon a comprehensive theoretical analysis of such phenomena. Competing theoretical orientations tend to be selective in what they take into account. Yet the educator is faced with the task of guiding a child's intellectual growth, and it is assumed that all that this entails is well understood.

Until the last decade, efforts to describe the nature of intellectual development were stymied by the philosophical dictum that only that which is directly observable, and therefore measurable, can be dealt with meaningfully. Thus, speculation about how the mind functions, about inner processes of thinking which are not directly observable, were deemed inadmissible. Psychologists' study of intellectual functioning was largely limited to the assessment of knowledge and the acquisition of particular skills. Intellectual functioning was defined in terms of accomplishments—facts learned, ability to perform, and other measurable entities. This posture emphasized the products of learning; it dealt with demonstrable changes in measurable behavior. The degree to which the criterion of measurability dominated methodology is revealed by the fact that intelligence was defined as "whatever an intelligence test measures." Knowledge of the growth of intellect was derived from the record of variation in performance on standardized tests by children of different ages.

In the late 1950s, however, with the renewed interest in Piaget's work, speculation about the workings of the mind suddenly became acceptable. Piaget's interest in children's reflections, their ways of ordering the world around them, his examination of the conceptual basis of intellectual performance opened the door to a study of cognitive process as well as of intellectual achievement. Jerome Bruner's research and theoretical analysis of children's thinking helped to solidify this new trend by building a bridge between cognitive psychology and experimental psychology. The adoption of what may be termed a cognitive perspective has set the stage for considerable theoretical speculation, including of course Piaget's extensive contributions, but no comprehensive, universally acceptable theoretical analysis of the nature of intellectual development has yet been put forth.

Thus, the educator of young children is being asked to promote a developmental process which is understood only incompletely. The field of cognitive development is advancing, but its path is not readily discernible. This chapter outlines some of the principal strands of this progress and examines how current trends in early childhood education reflect the diversity of thinking regarding the nature of intellectual development.

THE PSYCHOMETRIC VIEW

Until comparatively recently, the study of intellectual functioning simply entailed identifying and measuring abilities. Since the analysis of data was primarily directed toward achieving reliable quantification, the work was left to the hands of psychometricians. The basic data were test scores and item performance, and the crucial task has been to order and classify scores, to quantify how much ability or knowledge was achieved, and to study the relationship among different abilities. It was assumed that a test format with objective scoring of multiple items provided the only viable route to efficient assessment. The goal has been to arrive at a comprehensive description of the intellectual domain and to characterize the organization of abilities. L. L. Thurstone's pioneering study of primary mental abilities and the more recent efforts of J. P. Guilford constitute two of the most notable examples of this old but still thriving mode of investigation.[1] While this approach has its roots in the early tradition of measurement and classification of basic elements which characterized much of nineteenth-century European psychology, it has been compatible with the American school of behaviorism in that its theoretical speculation is cautious and empirically based, and it has always dealt with observables.

A major issue posed by this useful and necessary concern with measurement is the status assigned to measurability. Is the essence of a psychological thing defined by the way it is measured? Does its very existence depend on its measurability because a thing is nothing but how it is measured? Or, do we regard theoretical constructs as having a reality apart from their measures, and view the task of measurement as an evolutionary process of approximation in which succeeding measures gradually approach the essential character of what it is they are serving to quantify? According to the first viewpoint, measurement dominates a phenomenon; it determines its essence. In the second, measurement is seen as enhancing a concept by contributing to its usability, but, at the same time, its fallibility is acknowledged.

Given the need for reliable and efficient measurement, another premise developed: tests constitute the only viable means of assessment. Intellectual functioning came to be known as something measurable by tests, and attention turned to the improvement of tests. The standards of excellence were those tests that already existed, and the value of new instruments could gain acceptance only by demonstrating that they were capable of measuring with greater precision or efficiency, or provided a more differentiated assessment, than existing tests.

Piaget's use of the clinical interview and the recent refinement of observation methods have shown that other sources of information can be effectively used to assess intellectual functioning. Other considerations, as well, have helped to nudge tests off their pedestal. The cultural bias of tests, long known, is now much more widely regarded as a serious methodological defect. In addition, tests are much less appropriate for use with young children, and the rapid growth of early education has turned attention to the measurement needs of this field.

Further, the infallibility of the test paradigm has been challenged by psychometricians themselves. In their advocacy of construct validity as the major psychometric criterion, Jane Loevinger, and more recently Samuel Messick, have come to regard tests as tools for the elucidation of theoretical constructs and test scores as indexes rather than precise measures of these constructs.[2] Thus, tests have declined in status from a position wherein they defined the essence of intellectual functioning to serving as an auxiliary tool. The psychometric approach to the study of intellectual functioning, which evolved within a pragmatic, atheoretical outlook in which considerations of precise and efficient measurement held sway, seems now on its way to being reconstructed to function in the service of a theoretically oriented psychology.

The results of psychometric assessment affect policy decisions, and indirectly influence what is taught in the classroom. With increasing emphasis being placed on the accountability of educational programs and the need to evaluate innovative programs, the results of evaluation studies based on psychometric measurement of achievement determine which programs will be funded. A number of major educational research studies which have relied on psychometric assessment of educational progress have had a far-reaching impact on educational policy. Benjamin Bloom's demonstration that intellectual measures at age five correlate highly with those obtained during the final phases of formal education led to a reexamination of the importance of early development and public support for preschool education.[3] James Coleman's study of the effects of variation in educational opportunity forms much of the basis for the widespread skepticism toward the value of compensatory education and school integration.[4]

The air of authority and definitiveness with which such findings are presented tends to obscure the limited faith that researchers actually have in the validity of their measures and to brush aside questions regarding their relevance. Instead, the content of achievement tests is often mistakenly interpreted by practitioners as signifying precisely what analysts of the educational process regard as the essential substance of educational objectives. As a result, test content is gradually incorporated into the curriculum and assigned highest priority.

THE BEHAVIORIST POSITION

Until the 1960s most experimental psychological studies of intellectual functioning were guided by a behavioristic perspective. Its primary objective was to reduce the analysis of psychological phenomena to explicit, definable, and observable behavior. Keenly aware of the futility of mentalistic speculation, behaviorists were concerned with specifying the behaviors to be affected by a given transaction and with describing its dynamics in terms of manipulable stimulus-response linkages. The study of intellectual functioning was restricted to the analysis of the acquisition of specific responses. Behaviorists have preferred to deal with the concept of learning, defined by them as entailing a change in behavior, rather than with a mentalistic concept like intellectual functioning. Explanation of behavior proceeded in terms of the formation of stimulus-response connections by means of conditioning. Most studies dealt with simple forms of animal learning that easily fit into a stimulus-response paradigm and with those aspects of verbal learning which clearly involved discrete stimuli and responses. When called upon to explain more complex forms of intellectual functioning, the basic theoretical construct of stimulus-response linkage has been adapted to take into account the formation of implicit, mediating associations. The behavioristic analysis of discrimination learning experiments perhaps best illustrates how this method attempts to deal with more complex phenomena (see especially Kendler and Kendler).[5] Harold Stevenson's overview of the extensive but inconclusive research literature emphasizes how ill equipped the conceptual framework of behaviorism is to deal with any but the simplest instances of behavior.[6]

Another important tributary of behavioristic investigation has been the adaptation of Skinner's concept of operant conditioning to behavior analysis. This procedure demonstrates how behavior may be molded by the systematic application of the principle of reinforcement — that the probability of emitting a specific response can be increased by making the receipt of a reward contingent upon its execution. This method and its areas of application are more fully described in Chapter 9.

The behavioristic approach to intellectual functioning is closely linked to measurement. Its principal concern is with explicitness and observability. Since behaviorists emphasize the palpable behavioral changes to be effected by teaching, and are dissatisfied with accounts of education which refer to modifications of nonvisible states, they are interested in those aspects of education which deal with training. The design of workbooks, programmed instruction materials, and other procedures, which are mainly concerned with making explicit the particular responses to be learned and with orderng and sequencing the presentation of stimulus material to maximize the efficiency of learning, reflects the influence of the stimulus-response association orientation of behaviorist psychologists. The systematic application of behavior analysis has provided techniques for controlling maladaptive classroom behavior of individual children and led to the development of incentive systems that serve to motivate children and facilitate classroom management.

PIAGET'S COGNITIVE THEORY

Clearly the most significant influence upon current theoretical speculation about children's thinking has been the work of Piaget.[7] By demonstrating the active, constructive quality of children's thought, he has helped to quash the persistent though unarticulated belief that children learn by simply passively absorbing experienced stimulation. More than anyone else, Piaget has moved current thinking about the growth of the mind from the idea that it is a cerebral sponge which accumulates knowledge and conceptual content by mere exposure to the cognitive elements to a notion of the mind as an interacting agent which functions by inquiring, integrating, and synthesizing. The concept of intellectual growth as entailing accrual of informational content has been replaced by a theoretical framework which emphasizes the integrative aspects of cognitive development.

Equally important has been Piaget's speculation regarding the evolving character of a child's method of processing environmental stimulation. The stages of intellectual development postulated by Piaget have identified landmarks in the evolution of conceptual schema by which the mind apprehends reality. Piaget asks that we look at how the child acts upon experience in order to understand his way of thinking. He reminds us that the child's perspective in assessing environmental stimulation and his method of ordering experience themselves change with development.

Piaget's influence on educators has been significant. Perhaps most important, he provided the articulation of a theory, along with tentative evidence of its validity, which made provision for the type of mentalistic speculation which behaviorists eschewed. Educators who had been dissatisfied with restricting their formulation of goals and procedures to concrete behavioral acts and intuitively groped for a vocabulary and a theoretical sanction to engage in speculation about interior thought processes welcomed his contribution. Piaget's writings have led to an emphasis upon the cultivation of logical reasoning, on the ability to think as opposed to the learning of specific academic skills.

Piaget's contention that intellectual growth proceeds by the child's interaction with environmental stimulation has been interpreted as providing additional verification of the value of active learning, of the need for the role of initiative and personal experience in early learning. Conversely, it has implied that there are severe limits to the amount of passive learning that can be expected from young children. In addition, Piaget's delineation of the distinctive characteristics of logical reasoning associated with the various stages of cognitive development calls attention to the need for age-appropriate subject matter and media for learning in children.

Basing his research largely on a reformulation of Piaget's main ideas, Jerome Bruner mounted a program of study in cognitive development which graphically demonstrated the way in which research and education could be accommodated to a cognitive psychology. Bruner's cognitive studies with children emphasize how developmental changes in cognition can frequently be understood in terms of the growth of modes of information processing.[8] He focuses on how children handle information. Not surprisingly, his ideas about strategies of education emphasize active and integrative aspects of the learning process. Less rooted in a specific theoretical structure than is Piaget, Bruner has been more willing to apply his eclectic approach to a consideration of educational policy issues.[9]

COGNITIVE STYLE

The study of cognitive style represents a response to long-standing conflicts over whether psychological analysis should focus on form or content, product or process, qualitative or quantitative distinctions. The notion that it may be more useful to observe regularities in formal aspects of people's behavior, in how they function rather than the magnitude of their achievement, is at least as old as the beginnings of Gestalt psychology. A tradition of research has evolved which focuses on the way in which cognitive tasks are performed, on stylistic characteristics of performance rather than on effectiveness of functioning. It is based on the belief that variation in intellectual functioning can be better explained in terms of distinctive patterns of performance than by simply ordering people in terms of the magnitude of success/failure.

Among the most prominent distinctions in cognitive style are Herman Witkins' investigation of field dependence/independence and the concept of psychological differentiation, and Jerome Kagan's exploration of reflective/impulsive patterns of functioning.[10] Witkin examines how an individual performs in response to the task of adjusting a rod to the vertical position. He is concerned not simply with accuracy of judgment but with the kinds of cues (external versus internal) the subject chooses to use in making his perceptual judgment. Kagan studies the speed of an individual's response to a sorting task. He examines the latency of response rather than accuracy. Both investigators focus on how an individual goes about solving a problem rather than on the amount of success actually achieved.

Despite their intrinsic appeal, measures of cognitive style have not gained wide acceptance. They often fail to achieve acceptable levels of reliability and claims for validity are difficult to substantiate. One may always question whether the groups judged to be different in style really owe their distinctiveness to their stylistic identity or to factors which can be defined in terms other than style. Nevertheless, this work continues to arouse interest because it identifies dimensions of variation that are not indicated by conventional methods of assessment. It serves to highlight individual uniqueness rather than effectiveness; it contributes to the differentiation of individuality.

Some investigators believe that, once they are able to identify each individual's distinctive pattern of learning, it will be possible to accelerate education by utilizing each individual's preferred and more effective methods of acquiring and processing information. The study of cognitive style is also viewed as a means of identifying underdeveloped and underutilized modes of learning in each child, as a method for diagnosing and correcting impaired learning patterns. In assessing the use of a cognitive-style perspective in evaluation and guidance, Witkin points out that such characterizations tend to avoid good-bad and competent-deficient distinctions.[11] Thus a portrayal in terms of cognitive-style variables will be less threatening; it is less likely to meet with resistance. In addition, cognitive-style variables tend to focus on nonverbal domains. They provide an assessment of cognition which is quite independent of verbal skills; they are more likely to be free of the cultural bias which permeates the verbal content of most assessment methods.

Before applying the concept of cognitive style, the educator needs to obtain the answers to a series of questions which research has as yet only been able to answer partially. Taking Kagan's concept of impulsiveness/reflectiveness as an example, we would need to have the following clarified. Is there solid evidence of the generality of this trait, i.e., do children who display more impulsiveness on one task respond similarly on other tasks as well? Does this dimension of style really measure something different from effective performance — that is, do children who function more or less reflectively not necessarily perform more or less effectively? If style is found to be related to effective performance, is it the child's style which is responsible for his effectiveness or is it an accompaniment rather than a cause of effectiveness? And finally, can a child's style be modified in a way which will influence effectiveness of performance? Is cognitive style a malleable trait?

THE HOLISTIC PERSPECTIVE

Most conceptions of intellectual functioning have in common the fact that they are concerned with showing how it is distinct from other forms of behavior. At the same time, there has been an opposite tension. Instead of striving to define the separateness of intellectual behavior, other theorists have aimed at demonstrating its interdependence with all other forms of psychological functioning. They view intellectual behavior as representing one aspect, so defined for the sake of convenience, of a system which functions holistically and organismically. The Gestalt theorists, early in the history of psychology, were preoccupied with discrediting the prevailing atomism of psychology, the fragmentation which they viewed as distorting the essential interrelatedness of psychological phenomena. Heinz Werner compiled the existing evidence for an organismic psychology of intellectual development and became one of its leading theorists.[12]

But the organismic view seemed for years to serve only as a counterpoint to the prevailing concern for analyzing and measuring. Efforts to establish an organismic psychology have often been misunderstood and subjected to distortion. While Piaget appears to be almost exclusively concerned with logical and intellectual aspects of psychological functioning, his theoretical framework is nevertheless basically holistic. Yet, his theory seems to owe some of its appeal to the fact that it contains elements which can be assimilated into an atomistic methodology. Test items geared to measure a child's knowledge of conservation, transitivity, and other concepts introduced by Piaget have been assembled to augment the list of discrete abilities assessed by the psychometrician. "Piagetian curricula" have been devised for early childhood education programs which call for the training of children in exercises composed of Piagetian concepts. Despite their apparently distinctive Piagetian content, the mode of instruction and the theoretical orientation which guide the development of such training programs are at variance with Piaget's holistic viewpoint. Similarly, the study of cognitive style was initiated by proponents of an organismic theoretical viewpoint, but its major findings are often adapted to fit into an elementaristic trait psychology. Paths of research forged out of a commitment to the study of complexity tend to be rerouted into the mainstream of atomistic thinking.

During the past two decades, the focus of most research in cognitive functioning has continued to be on differentiating its nature rather than clarifying how it is integrated with other behaviors. Nevertheless, this issue continues to surface. Michael Cole and Sylvia Scribner, in a recent survey of what has been learned from cross-cultural studies of cognition, observe that most data are based upon a specific method of interrogation using standard laboratory stimuli and data-gathering situations.[13] Because of the highly circumscribed character of investigation of the cognitive domain—the methods, content of material and situations employed—they conclude that most findings lack the generality often implied by their authors. Addressing themselves to the question of cultural differences in cognition, Cole and Scribner find little evidence for clear-cut, across-the-board differences between groups in particular cognitive skills. When there are differences, they can usually be explained in terms of the particular methods used and the situations in which the data were gathered.

In the course of their cultural comparisons of cognition, Cole and Scribner come to question a basic methodological premise of most research in cognition—that each cognitive task can be subjected to analysis in order to identify precisely the cognitive elements that it comprises and then, in turn, that each of its component abilities can be assessed in absolute terms. Instead, they propose that Luria's concept of a functional cognitive system be invoked to achieve the most valid description of cognitive phenomena. Since most complex cognitive tasks entail a multitude of processes, all of which are sensitive to the configuration of conditions under which they are evoked and to the interplay among them, Cole and Scribner conclude that it is more useful to conceive of cognitive behaviors in functional terms rather than to view them as palpable, precisely measurable physical entities. They expect to find and understand cultural differences in cognition at the level of functional systems of cognition rather than in terms of component cognitive processes. In a similar vein, I concluded from a study of conservation of number that, contrary to expectations, studies of cognition seldom tell us whether or not a child has a particular skill, they do not provide data regarding the presence/absence of a specific cognitive ability. They reveal, instead, something about the conditions under which the child may use the ability in question.[14]

Similarly, Cole and Scribner are not ready to take performance on a given set of test items or problem-solving situations at face value. They do not accept the premise of the psychometrician that a well-constructed set of test items constitutes a definitive method for revealing the presence or absence of a particular skill or fact. Rather they view the presentation of a given set of items as having the potential for activating a whole system of interpretation and response to the test situation. It may not be assumed that the child's response is directly related to the specific characteristics of the items themselves. For Cole and Scribner, administration of a particular cognitive task becomes the occasion for revealing something about how the respondent organizes and interprets the total situation. They are more concerned with learning about a child's organizational framework, with the circumstances under which he interprets questions in different ways, with the different strategies that are used in conjunction with different interpretations of a task, and with the various conditions under which children can use relevant information in their possession to solve a particular problem.

Another expression of the organismic viewpoint is found in the work of Barbara Biber, Edna Shapiro, and David Wickens who present strategies for promoting cognitive growth from a developmental-interaction point of view.[15] They list among their educational goals for the preschool years ". . . to help the child internalize impulse control, to meet the child's need to cope with conflicts intrinsic to this stage of development, to facilitate the development of an image of self as an unique and competent person, and to help the child establish mutually supporting patterns of interaction." Thus, they define the main problem-solving activities of the preschool child largely in terms of mastery of impulse life, resolution of conflicts, clarification of self-image, and learning how to relate to others. In this formulation the fusion of cognitive and affective aspects of psychological functioning becomes apparent. The tasks of early learning focus on emotional and social phenomena — with observing the regularities of feeling states and managing their expression, with understanding the incompatibility between certain goals and/or modes of behaving, with integrating information about the self into a coherent and stable image, and with learning to recognize the needs of others and reconcile them with pursuing one's own goals in a social situation. Implicit in this formulation is the fundamental unity of emotion and thought, long regarded as a basic tenet of ego psychology, but absent among those who have studied intellectual functioning from an academic research perspective. It is only recently that substantial numbers of investigators of cognitive development have begun to show interest in the cognitive content of a child's social interaction and emotional life.[16]

The contrasting views of intellectual functioning described here can be at least partly understood as reflecting alternative ways of dealing with complexity. The main task of research is most often viewed as that of confirming with a much greater degree of certainty what was previously only surmised to be true. This notion restricts research to the familiar and places the principal burden on its ability to generate definitive evidence. Most research methodology owes its character to this concern and, in turn, most researchers have adopted this outlook. When faced with phenomena that involve a multiplicity of variables, this viewpoint advocates cutting the problem down to size and limiting it to the part about which one can be certain.

In sharp contrast is a stance which views the complexity of a system as its main attribute and avoids dissection into parts for fear that its essential character will be destroyed. Research is viewed as being directed toward elaborating and clarifying complexity, with yielding a more differentiated, fuller description of a phenomenon, rather than analyzing it into simpler, more understandable parts.

In their single-minded concern for achieving certainty, most re-searchers attend only to that aspect of behavior which seems to be amenable to productive study. To establish certainty regarding any issue, however narrowly defined, is a demanding and time-consuming task. The researcher is accustomed to postponing dealing with what he does not understand until another time. The nature of his work virtu-ally dictates the adoption of a perspective of fragmentation.

Whereas research psychologists have had difficulty coming to terms with an organismic theory of intellectual functioning, many educators find this position congenial. Perhaps it is their clinical perspective which attracts educators to this viewpoint. The educator and clinician are forced to confront the complexity of a total psychological system. In one way or another they are required to look at children holistical-ly. As children grow older, it may be possible to view them exclusively as solvers of algebra problems or as learners of conversational French. But when they are young, and individuation of intellectual function-ing has barely begun, the fluidity of children's behavior demands that they be looked at from an organismic viewpoint.

The objective of this chapter has been to provide an overview of the major currents of thought concerned with describing and explaining the nature of intellectual functioning in children. The diversity of conceptual systems is extensive and accounts for the disarray which educators find when they seek an authoritative analysis of this seem-ingly familiar and well-understood topic. The range of variation of contrasting explanatory constructs extends from a basically elemen-taristic notion which views intellectual functioning as simply the sum total of visible behaviors which result from previous experience. Each discrete response is seen as connected to and activated by a stimulus element or a network of sequenced stimulus-response linkages. A giant switchboard is envisaged as the mechanism for routing and coordinat-ing the mass of message units to be stored and activated at the appro-priate time. The management of intellectual functioning consists largely of ordering the bits of behavior to be learned and arranging for the proper sequence of stimulus presentation.

At the opposite end of this continuum are theoretical frameworks that focus, not on the visible array of behaviors to be changed but on the internal, non-visible, hypothetical integrative mechanisms which give direction and power to intellectual functioning. Of the theorists concerned with the central, organizing function of thought, Bruner is most closely attuned to the concept of a switchboard operation which monitors the flow of information. His research has focused on information-processing behavior in order to begin to characterize the nature of the nonvisible switchboard apparatus.

Most other theoretical concerns with integrative mechanisms have been less interested in accommodating to the elementaristic and behavioristic conception of psychological phenomena. Piaget, an epistemologist, has described the evolving stages of schema which guide children's way of understanding reality. Werner, in his concern with the unified, integrating superstructure of psychological systems, was devoted to clarifying the nature of development from an organismic standpoint. Cole and Scribner, having begun with dimensional analysis of discrete behaviors not unlike the functionalist-behaviorist tradition of experimental psychology, have become sensitized to the role of superordinate organizational systems as influencing response patterns to specific stimuli. The work of Biber, Shapiro, and Wickens reminds us that integrative mechanisms need to contend with the continuous interaction between cognitive and affective elements of psychological functioning.

At the level of measurement, we have the psychometric tradition which has as its cornerstone the recording and assessment of individual differences. It assigns importance to data only insofar as it records variation in response, and the precise measurement of that variation is regarded as the only psychological reality. This assumption has been attacked from within as well as without the psychometric world. Advocates of construct validity view measurement as a means to a theoretical end and not as an end in itself. On the other hand, investigators of cognitive style begin with the premise that the most interesting characteristics are those which distinguish among the performance of individuals whose conventional quantitative scores are the same.

These extremely diverse, sometimes contradictory, conceptions of what is important about intellectual functioning and how it develops tend to flourish and grow in settings especially designed to accommodate to their perspective. Each helps to clarify various aspects and elements of a complex process, but the scope of the work, and perhaps more important, the outlook that governs it, are often defined by criteria that are different from those of the educator. Yet we persist in viewing the researcher as leading the way for the educator. The narrow beam of the research light sometimes illuminates areas which are crucial to the educator; at other times it provides only flashes which do not even provide a hint of the complexity which needs to be understood. The educator is exposed to a much broader and diversified range of intellectual functioning. It would seem that he should be viewed more as the source and the collaborator, rather than as client and beneficiary of research into intellectual functioning.

Notes

1. Leon L. Thurstone, *Primary Mental Abilities,* Psychometric Monographs No. 1 (Chicago: University of Chicago Press, 1938); Joy P. Guilford, *The Nature of Human Intelligence* (New York: McGraw-Hill, 1967).

2. Jane Loevinger, "Objective Tests as Instruments of Psychological Theory," Monograph Supplement 9, *Psychological Reports* 3 (December 1957): 635-694; Samuel Messick, "The Standard Problem: Meaning and Values in Measurement and Evaluation," *American Psychologist* 30 (October 1975): 955-966.

3. Benjamin S. Bloom, *Stability and Change in Human Characteristics* (New York: John Wiley & Sons, 1964).

4. James Coleman, *Equality of Educational Opportunity* (Washington, D.C.: U.S. Government Printing Office, 1966).

5. See especially Tracy S. Kendler, Howard H. Kendler, and Martha Carrick, "Verbal Labels and Inferential Problem Solution of Children," *Child Development* 37 (December 1966): 749-763.

6. Harold W. Stevenson, "Learning in Children," in *Carmichael's Manual of Child Psychology,* Vol. I, ed. Paul H. Mussen, 3d ed. (New York: John Wiley & Sons, 1970), 859-938.

7. Jean Piaget, "Piaget's Theory," *ibid.,* 703-732; *id.* and Barbel Inhelder, *The Psychology of the Child* (New York: Basic Books, 1970); H. Ginsburg and S. Opper, *Piaget's Theory of Intellectual Development: An Introduction* (Englewood Cliffs, N.J.: Prentice-Hall, 1969).

8. Jerome S. Bruner, R. R. Olver, and P. M. Greenfield, *Studies in Cognitive Growth* (New York: John Wiley & Sons, 1966).

9. Jerome S. Bruner, *The Process of Education* (Cambridge, Mass.: Harvard University Press, 1960).

10. Herman A. Witkin *et al., Personality through Perception: An Experimental and Clinical Study* (Westport, Conn.: Greenwood Press, 1972; originally published by Harper & Brothers in 1954); *id. et al., Psychological Differentiation: Studies of Development* (Potomac, Md.: Lawrence Erlbaum Associates, 1974; originally published by John Wiley & Sons in 1962); Jerome Kagan *et al., Information Processing in the Child: Significance of Analytic and Reflective Attitudes,* Monograph No. 578, *Psychological Monographs* 78 (No. 1, 1964).

11. Herman A. Witkin, "A Cognitive-Style Perspective on Evaluation and Guidance," in *Proceedings of the 1973 Invitational Conference on Testing Problems-Measurement for Self-Understanding and Personal Development* (Princeton, N.J.: Educational Testing Service, 1973).

12. Heinz Werner, *Comparative Psychology of Mental Development* (New York: International Universities Press, 1948).

13. Michael Cole and Sylvia Scribner, *Culture and Thought: A Psychological Introduction* (New York: John Wiley & Sons, 1974).

14. Herbert Zimiles, *The Development of Conservation and Differentiation of Number,* Monograph No. 108, *Monographs of the Society for Research in Child Development* 31 (No. 6, 1966).

15. Barbara Biber, Edna Shapiro, and David Wickens in collaboration with Elizabeth Gilkeson, *Promoting Cognitive Growth: A Developmental-Interaction Point of View* (Washington, D.C.: National Association for the Education of Young Children, 1971).

16. David J. Bearison and Thomas Z. Cassel, "Cognitive Decentration and Social Codes: Communicative Effectiveness in Young Children from Differing Family Contexts," *Developmental Psychology* 11 (No. 1, 1975): 29–36.

4. Cognition in Early Childhood Education: A Historical Perspective

Barbara Biber

The place of cognition in early childhood education programs has moved into and out of focus during this century. In part, this reflects changing psychological theory as well as an increase in information concerning thinking processes gained as the result of experimental studies. It is also tied to contrasting views of man and the near and far goals of education. It is very much affected by social issues and by inferences as to how cognitive power or the lack of it is causally related to them.[1]

I see cognition from two perspectives: the first reflects the century-long evolution of design and philosophy in early childhood education; the second is influenced by relatively recent programs developed in response to social crisis and controversial social demands. Newer programs, largely under governmental aegis, have drawn increasingly on the field of psychology—itself a field in controversy.

Long-term educational program development has been pejoratively labeled "establishment," "traditional," and other such terms indicating resistance to change. Conversely, to experienced educators many newly structured programs appear unseasoned in quality and restricted in scope because most psychologists were newcomers to the world of early education, albeit that what they produced had the charm as

well as the faults of "brain children." Evelyn Weber's terminology
seems least argumentative.[2] She refers to centurylong developments as
"mainstream," a term that honors the wisdom that comes from continuous doing and undoing and, at the same time, suggests that there
is something beyond. Here I concentrate on one major aspect of the
educational process, namely, changes in theory and practice that are
associated with shifting and differing ways of thinking about thinking.
Some of these changes can be traced continuously along the path of
the "mainstream"; others appear sporadically, in connection with the
short-term programs developed in response to social pressures, the
crisis of war, fears of weakened national standing, and awakened
social conscience about class and ethnic inequalities.

FROM THE TWENTIES TO THE FORTIES: DIVERGENT TRENDS

John B. Watson: Behaviorism Applied

Between the years 1920 and 1940, approximately, the two major
controversial positions that confront us today were in the making.
There was Watsonian behaviorist theory with its image of a relatively
passive organism, largely predetermined potential, and a theory of
learning built on stimulus-response connections and the influence of
specific conditioning factors. It was from this perspective that habit-
training came to have a central position in learning; at the younger
levels, in many preschools, the focus of education was on activities that
were called "routines" for many years. In order to establish good
habits at an early age, the functions of eating, sleeping, and elimina-
tion were carefully planned and supervised. But, since the human race
has a way of saving itself from theories, psychological ones included,
the children played and were inevitably cognitively engaged. Opportunity for play, including both the setting and the materials, was provided, but the investment in and the assessment of learning was in
other spheres. In Eveline Omwake's words: "There were black marks
on the record of any beginning teacher who let a child sit on a chair so
high his feet couldn't be flat on the floor or so low that the knees were
at too high an angle. In the twenties and thirties routines were all as
tightly structured and carefully planned as the most precise programmed language concept learning series today but playtime was left up
to the children and they were free to engage in it whenever they
weren't eating, sleeping, going to the toilet. . ."[3]

John Dewey: Guiding Theory

It was still the 1920s — 1929 to be exact — when I walked into Harriet Johnson's nursery room on the top floor of the City and Country School in the Greenwich Village area of New York City.[4] I was a green psychologist on a first job with a fresh pad in my hand, assigned to observe and record the drawing activities of the children, aged eighteen months to three years.[5] That was another world of learning. It represented the opposing trend at the time. Those who inherited that dichotomy are now described in textbooks under the heading, "behavioristic versus phenomenalistic view of man."

Multiple forces, social and personal, determined the climate, the curriculum, and the tone of that nursery room. Essentially, it was the thinking of John Dewey that was the core of educational theory.[6] General precepts and methods, developed for the primary and elementary years, were adapted to these early formative years. Dewey's hopes for positive social change were invested, in large measure, in educating a thinking man. If there were to be intelligent activity in the end, that is, foresight based on observation, information, and judgment, there had to be active thinking in the formative years. The ways of schooling were to be radically different from the past. It was a challenge to provide a learning environment rich in possibilities for direct contact and interaction with things, people, and ideas — one in which emerging symbolic skills would gain salience by being tested, tried out, and enjoyed in natural functional contexts. For older children this led to the project method in curriculum; for younger ones, the emphasis was on communicating with other people in gesture or words or capturing meaning through nonverbal rehearsal of experience in expressive and play form.

The Harriet Johnson Nursery School; the Progressive School Movement

It is important to remember that the nursery school, as part of the active progressive school movement, was directly influenced by Dewey's thinking. In that sense, it differed from other models of education in early childhood that were more influenced by social welfare trends and behavioristic psychology. Looking back, one asks what place, in this context, did the goal of honing the cognitive processes have in the program and what specific methods were intended to serve that goal? I shall limit myself to this one situation. A complete answer would require the examination of other lower schools or progressive schools or independent nursery schools aligned with the Dewey philosophy.

"Thinking" does not appear as a heading in the table of contents for Harriet Johnson's *Children in the Nursery School*,[7] in which she presented recorded observations of the children and explained the rationale for the program that she called an "intentionally planned environment." But her clear interest in children's thinking and the teacher's role in stimulating it appear as integral parts of descriptions of physical-motor activities, dramatic play, social interactions, and the use of materials for construction. In each content area she documented progressive stages from early sensory-motor, manipulative activity to the capacity to deal symbolically with experience. She took the kind of records of behavior that are once more being recognized as basic material for analysis of behavior and interaction. The teacher's role was to nourish the sensory-motor skills of the early stages by providing a variety of experiences carefully selected to be within the child's capacity for satisfying, self-initiated action and interaction. She was concerned that the manipulative, sensory-motor activities be well supported and recognized as foundation for the symbolic stage into which these young children were moving.

She regarded the self-initiated, experimental play use of materials as a prime medium for learning and defined the teacher's role accordingly. The teacher was expected to be aware of and responsive to a child's building of a boat with blocks and boards, and his lusty call "All a bore! All a bore!" as he called the others to join him. She saw it as a conceptual configuration while she phrased it in the simple vernacular of "organized knowledge." The salient role in stimulating thinking, in moving the children toward more comprehensive conceptual schemata, shows up in a record in which she offers the child a wheel to incorporate into his dramatic play. Whether or not he accepts it is a complex matter, but the possibility and the option to refuse are open to him. This is one instance of the myriad occasions in which the teacher was expected to move thinking toward more advanced levels in ways sensitive to what has since been called the problem of the "match."

Not only the special activity of self-initiated play but also the ongoing experience of life in the schoolroom were continuously used to stimulate the children toward sharpened perception, toward organizing experience along dimensions of similarity and difference, toward seeing objects in terms of their functional attributes. This shows up in the record of a child standing with the teacher, looking out the window and listening to the sounds coming through. The teacher's verbalization with the child merges the differentiating process with rhythmic sound elements. "Clop-clop . . . that's horse! Rattley-rattle, that's an old cart! Sh-sh-sh, honk, honk, that's a taxicab." The salient differentiation of self from others was invested in chants about "Yvonne's daddy, George's daddy, Caleb's daddy," or about colors distinguished by a song about each child's sweater. Putting on sweaters to go outdoors was not left in the barren state of being a routine act; the teacher offered the answer to an unasked question when she remarked, "It's cold outside." The child's spoken questions were likely to be used as the means of helping him find his own answers.

Child: "What that nail in kiddie car for?"
Teacher: "You tell me."
Child: "So handle won't come off. Why handle don't come off for?"
Teacher: "You know, Walter, you tell me."
Child: "So Walter can ride," he said, with a big smile and a chuckle of enjoyment.

The egocentric ending, natural to the stage of development, does not diminish the fun of engaging with the teacher in a joust of "why" thinking.

Commitment to the dimension of thinking in early childhood education did not take the form of exercises to reinforce cognitive processes of differentiation, classification, or causal thinking. It was expressed, rather, in a systematic effort to create a learning environment in which conceptual organization of elements of experience — schemata for perceiving and formulating relationships — would be continuously and naturally stimulated as part of the child's encounter, physical and symbolic, in the course of his active response to his environment.

I have been quoting Harriet Johnson and her work with children not yet three years old. For a fuller picture of the salient place of cognition in this educational atmosphere, I would have to draw on material describing work with the children in the later nursery years and into the primary years. Here I can only briefly refer to Caroline Pratt's insight into the use of blocks as material for thinking in space,[8] and to Lucy Mitchell's principle of stimulating "relationship thinking" as a prime purpose for incorporating the study of the environment, from the earliest years, into the curriculum design.[9] Another illustration was Irma Black's way of describing to parents, in writing for the newspaper, *PM*, and *Parents' Magazine* in 1941, how a cooking experience with children can be made a way of storing up diversified impressions of physical transformations and how these serve him well when he is ready to articulate his wonder in the form of questions about melting, freezing, and evaporation.[10]

Focus on Concept Formation

From my own files I can draw on a collection of "concept" records. At some time in the 1930s at the Harriet Johnson Nursery School I initiated a period in which teachers' regularly written records were restricted to observations of the children's thinking behavior, partly to gain some mastery over this attractive and challenging field for myself and partly to stimulate greater awareness on the part of the teachers. The material was systematized into cognitive processes and concept configurations and arrayed into what seemed to be characteristics of newfound clarity at successive age levels.

The following are just a few illustrations from the material about four- and five-year-old children. Under the heading, "understanding and interest in a changing, dynamic world," I find an entry concerned with the children's response to the story about "The Tree in the Forest."

Teacher: "What do they do when they want to cut down a tree in the forest?"
Wendy: "A man comes with an axe. He cuts off the leaves. Makes it white."
Teacher: "How does he make it white?"
Wendy: "He takes the coat off."
Sheldon: "It isn't called a coat, it's a . . . "
Paul: "It's bark."
Teacher: "What would they need trees for?"
Paul: "For wood."
Sheldon: "For building houses."
Paul: "Trees are round. How do they get flat?"
Craig: "There's a sawmill, it goes around, you shove the tree in and they saw it. It comes out all sawed."

Under another heading, "growing interest in extraperceptual phenomena and ability to think in alternatives," there appears an entry that originated with a conversation on the elevator.

The teacher, going back to the play roof with the children, pushed the wrong button, the third floor instead of the fourth, and then corrected her error. Henry: "Miss H, did you make a mistake in numbers, or did you forget and think you were going to the room instead of the roof?"

For the sake of a bit of personal history, let me add that certain books regularly disappeared from our library shelves: Jean Piaget's *Language and Thought of the Child*[11] and *Child's Conception of the World*,[12] along with Susan Isaac's *Intellectual Growth in Young Children*[13] and *Social Development in Young Children*.[14] I never knew whether the culprits were the teachers entranced by the program of recording children's thinking or the student teachers trying to understand why I thought it was so important to understand Isaacs' controversy with Piaget in our class on child development. It pleases me, if I am right, to sense a revived appreciation of Isaacs' contribution and recognition of full, uncoded record taking as an important experience for students.

Curriculum Principles

From this early period I think it is fair to say that we had three guiding principles for making curriculum decisions that gave the thinking processes high priority in the children's learning experience: (1) Play is a basic mode for thinking in early childhood. (2) An important aspect of the teacher's role is to exploit the ongoing daily encounters, physical and social, as material for stimulating thinking processes. (3) The cognitive search for relationships should be stimulated through providing varied, multiple opportunities for the children's direct, active contact with the people and processes of their environment.

THE FORTIES AND THE FIFTIES: THE POWER OF THE EMOTIONS

The Influence of Psychodynamic Theory

Alongside their highly motivated concern for finding optimal ways to stimulate intellectual development, there were some early childhood educators who had an equally strong commitment to understand children in terms of psychodynamic theories of development and personality and to mold educational practices accordingly. The seminal source was, of course, Freudian theory, but the nursery school world in America moved more toward a neo-Freudianism, with more attention to the impact of sociocultural influences and less emphasis on determinism.

New sensitivity to the undersurfaces of behavior, to the depth and power of emotional responsiveness became part of educational thinking and led to changes in the quality of experience in many classrooms. There was increased understanding of the inner struggles of growing up: the management of overwhelming emotion; feelings of ambivalence, conflict, and guilt in relationships with loved figures; the pull between impulse and adaptation, between the lingering comfort of dependence and the siren call of independence. Childhood was perceived as a period of emotional weathering of much pain alongside deep pleasure. There were significant changes in the way negative behavior was handled, in the materials and opportunities offered to help children express and resolve emotional problems, and, most important, in the nature of the teacher-child relationship.

In a paper on the "Fundamental Needs of the Child," Lawrence Frank presented an eloquent statement on the emotional turbulence of childhood and the implications for the teacher role.[15] In his statement he spoke for many of us—Caroline Zachary, Mary Shattuck Fisher, Lili Peller, Evelyn Beyer, Eveline Omwake, myself, and others—who had become convinced that a sound environment for young children had to be geared toward emotional health as well as toward cognitive strength. The place of self-initiated play gained increasing importance. We saw it as serving two different growth processes for the young child: the learning implicit in selecting and clarifying experience through self-directed reenactment and the release available through symbolic expression of burdensome fears and conflicts.

Beyond Montessori

This view of early childhood education, in which the thinking and feeling processes both claimed attention in the composition of the learning environment and in which play had a central place, was widely but not universally accepted in the preschool world. The rationale and implementation obviously run counter to the principles and practices of the Montessori system, which also gained prominence in this country at about the same time Montessori methods were highly structured to achieve skills and lacked concern for the emotional undercurrents of early childhood. Evelyn Beyer made the difference clear.[16]

THE SIXTIES: PSYCHOLOGISTS' INTEREST IN PRESCHOOL EDUCATION

Misreading of History

This is a good place to pause before I attempt to follow the path through the developments that were generated in the effort to undo the effects of poverty and discrimination. It has been a surprise to me to find repeated statements to the effect that interest in cognitive processes was a new development associated with the period in which compensatory programs were launched. The earlier period is said to have been entirely oriented toward physical, social, and emotional growth. In one investigator's opinion the child in the earlier period was viewed as being in a "state of mindlessness," and it was time to see him "not only as a reactor and a purposer but also as a knower." This view was mistaken and surprising to those of us who had been continuously trying to find ways to nurture emerging thought processes at the same time that we brought newer insights into the life of feeling and fantasy to bear on the total complex educational process.

There is more than one reason for this widespread misreading of history by many who have unimpeachable credentials as scholars. Certainly there was a great deal of variation in the way in which the philosophy and the associated educational goals of progressive-oriented schools were enacted, but there are other possible explanations for why academically trained psychologists might miss the important place thinking held in progressive programs. They may not have seen a proper sampling of schools in action or have known that they existed. They may not have recognized attention to cognitive processes when these did not appear as specifically structured lessons but were, instead, interwoven with the total experiential scheme of learning. To hail the discovery of a new continent that had already been discovered should be a little embarrassing. What is more important and more regrettable, however, is that, in trying to move ahead, old ground already plowed has had to be plowed again.

Inferences from Cognitive Theory

To encompass the busy, somewhat hectic years in the decade of the 1960s and since, I intend to separate the influence of some of the theoretical formulations of cognition from programs aimed at remedying the disadvantaged position of the poor and minority child population, attributed by most to cognitive deficit.

An Epistemological Formulation Interpreted for Education

From theory to practice is a complex process, as is evident from the variety of educational programs that claim their origins in the same theory. But there is no conscionable alternative to making the effort. From cognitive theory developmental psychologists drew inferences and made suggestions on desirable curriculum construction. Piaget's systematic analysis of the course of thinking—a monumental episte-mological work—has had increasing influence on early education, pointing in opposite directions from behaviorist theory.[17] If Ellis Evans is right,[18] this has been a surprise to Piaget, who had only three re-commendations: "provide children with actual objects to manipulate, assist children in their development of question-asking skills, and know why particular operations are difficult for children." The first two recommendations speak to how teachers should act: the last asks them to be students, or, better yet, scholars of childhood. Intended or not, Piaget has recognized the extent of his influence on education suf-ficiently to be motivated to correct misinterpretations, namely, the well-known American acceleration error. That reminds me of a paper John Dewey gave in 1938, in which he decried the misinterpretation of his theory.[19] He critizied the tendency to accept pleasure as a sufficient criterion for the worthwhileness of experience and to neglect the need for orderly organization of subject matter. Scholars, too, have their troubles.

For those of us who cross the professions of education and psychol-ogy, the positive reception of Piagetian theory in recent years by many psychologists interested in education has been a deeply satisfying experience. Without being so presumptuous as to claim that we had all those insights long ago, there is basis for seeing substantial congru-ence between the established implementation of progressive philos-ophy over the years and the inferences for practice now being drawn from Piaget. One example is the very learning-teaching principles of-fered by Evans as being implications to be drawn from Piagetian theory. They have been offered as abstract principles in progressive educational theory for many years.[20] Moreover, the rationale for which specific transactions in the life of the schoolroom are truest means for implementing these principles has appeared as an articulated body of empirical knowledge, expressed in a vast literature. Each principle that Evans names calls up an image of practice long since incorpo-rated as part of a comprehensive image built up over the years of what constitutes excellence in a learning atmosphere.

For his "active self-discovery," I see well-equipped situations with open schedules and an honest invitation to explore. For "inductive learning experience," I see experiences planned outside the classroom, such as trips and the Socratic-style group discussions that follow, for

"novel experiences facilitating stage-relevant thinking operations accommodated to the child's intellectual style," I see a group of four-
year-olds taking a new route through the building to their play roof,
internalizing the experience of alternative means to a common end.
For "enriched concrete sensory experience," I see the easels, the clay
boards, the musical instruments, the gerbil nibbling in his cage. For
"symbolization in manipulative play and aesthetic experience," I see
the complex block structures, the dress-up materials, the house play
corner. For the "sharing of viewpoints," I hear the teacher calming a
fight between two children as each presents her case verbally to the
other while at the same time helping them find an acceptable way to
deal with conflicting impulses. Many other parallels could be drawn.

Advance in understanding of cognitive processes in childhood
should and will lead to change in the pattern of the learning atmosphere and in modes of teaching. The shift from empirical formulation
to more generalized theorizing in itself represents invaluable progress
in a profession. The more "general" level of understanding opens the
door for more inventive, adaptive particularities in practice. But is it
too much to ask that scholars master the knowledge already gained
and integrate it with new directions for growth? Or is it too much to
ask that there be a long pause before methods for gaining knowledge
of psychological processes be translated literally into an educational
program?[21] This approach, which characterized Constance Kamii's
early expositions, has recently been retracted by her.[22] Her most recent
formulation bears significant resemblance to the developmental-
interaction point of view described later and to the educational practice derived therefrom.

The Fall of Fixed Intelligence

If we turn to other formulations, the inferences drawn from cognitive theory to education are varied, expressing different priorities for
one or another aspect of that theory. J. McVicker Hunt slew the
dragon of fixed intelligence and clarified in educational terms the
meaning of two of Piaget's somewhat idiosyncratic terms: assimilation
and accommodation.[23] By this thinking the teacher is expected to be
both a sensitive and an informed instrument — able to judge the nature
of integrative patterns already achieved by the child, able to select
from a rich repertoire of appropriate next steps in learning in an effort
to motivate the child, able to challenge forward movement without
imposing disabling stress or strain. It is through such repeated "matched"

learning experiences that given potential has an optimal chance to approach its limits.

Development as Aim

Lawrence Kohlberg and Rochelle Mayer move the issues on to a broader philosophical level.[24] The sequential evolution of thinking processes described by Piaget are taken by them to be the actual aims of education, not the instrumentality through which other goals are mediated. Ideally, in this view, education is the movement toward logical and ethical principles that are universals, transcending cultural variation. To support this developmental process, these authors turn to the progressivism of John Dewey with its emphasis on broad, open opportunity to construct, explore, express, play, and communicate. They express doubt that growth will be facilitated by specific training programs. In this system quite a wide variety of curricula are acceptable since the authors are not concerned with weighing the place of psychodynamic factors in the composition of the learning atmosphere.

Teacher Enactment

Millie Almy brings her understanding of Piagetian theory and the insights she has gained from her own experimental work right to the classroom. Her suggestions for applying Piagetian theory reveal intimate knowledge of the teacher's role as she indicates what older, established ways should be put aside and how newer ways can be introduced with flexibility. Almy claims that "Piaget's theory leaves no question as to the importance of learning through activity. Demonstrations, pictured illustrations, particularly for the youngest children, clearly involve the child less meaningfully than do his own manipulation and his own experimentation. While the vicarious is certainly not to be ruled out, it is direct experience that is the avenue of knowledge and logical ability."[25]

Movement toward Cognitive-Affective Theory

To many people, both theoreticians and practitioners, cognitive theory was stimulating, enlightening, and seminal. But for educators it was and is incomplete.[26] From different perspectives it has been recognized that the affective phenomena of human behavior have to be incorporated into the theoretical framework in order to provide adequate foundation for educational practice.

Competence: Objective and Subjective

In the mood of revising orthodox analytic theory, Robert White, like the cognitive theorists, emphasized how learning takes place through action and its consequences.[27] But in his system of thought there are two equally important orders of consequence. One has to do with the capacity to interact effectively with the environment, whether at the level of practicing motor skills or resolving problem situations with one's peers—in short, to be competent. The other is the subjective side of competence, the cumulative sense (conscious or unconscious) of one's own ability to be effective. To maintain this subjective sense of competence becomes an important nucleus of motivation for further engagement with the environment and leads, in a cycle, to new levels of competence.

Affect Deepening the Learning Experience

From quite another perspective, Richard Jones criticized the overemphasis on curriculum materials and cognitive proficiency and the corresponding underemphasis on emotional factors as these appeared in Jerome Bruner's "Man: A Course of Study."[28] He describes how the emotions aroused in the children by seeing a film on breast feeding, seal hunting, and other customs of the Netsilik Eskimos could and should have been utilized for deepening learning instead of being treated as obstructions to clear thinking.

I have selected just two examples, one by Robert White and the other by Richard Jones, from among others to show a change I seem to see in conceptualization of the cognitive and affective processes that took place between the 1940s and the 1960s. In the earlier period, as I mentioned, we had recognized the importance of understanding and providing for the fulfillment of emotional needs and the resolution of emotional conflicts, but our orientation was additive. We were saying to ourselves, consider not only the intellect but also the affect. By the 1960s the line of thinking had matured, and understanding the complex interaction of cognitive and affective processes became and remains the challenge.

Developmental and Psychodynamic Perception of Behavior

Understanding requires sensitive perception not only of what is before one's eyes but also of multiple simultaneous meanings inherent in child behavior. I once resorted to a metaphor, asking that adults learn to have a kind of binocular perception of the learning child, so that awareness of associated emotional processes could be as naturally and knowledgeably considered as intellectual gain. I tried to illustrate what I meant by presenting an image of a typical nursery school event:

To the outside eye, they are busy, active children enjoying themselves. To the conscious educator, they are learning new skills; [at the same time] they are accruing new knowledge of themselves. Not only a child but a new self-feeling swishes down the slide with outstretched arms after he has climbed to the top of the jungle gym for the first time and, standing alone, has scanned the endless vista of the neighboring roofs. He is gaining direct knowledge of the nature of the physical world, knowledge that, in a few years, will be transformed into abstract concepts of weight and pressure, of wheel and axle, of hoisting and leverage. The adults in this world echo the child's pleasure in the expanding sense of himself as he moves about in his physical world, and see in his playful elaboration of physical feats the evidence of his individuality, making over in his own shape the "world" he has been given.[29]

Description helps to communicate, but only analysis builds a tool. We need to build tools for our viewpoint.

In 1967 Margery Franklin and I made a systematic attempt, in brief form, to supply a framework for thinking of the preschool child's behavior in terms both of developmental and psychodynamic principles. We limited ourselves to six formulations, stated in general terms. For each one the discussion of the psychological processes was interwoven with implications for educational programs and made concrete with illustrations of behavioral events. One of the statements, representing the developmental view, reads: "An individual does not operate at a 'fixed' developmental level, but manifests in his behavior a range of genetically different aspirations. Earlier or more primitive modes of organization are not eradicated, but become integrated into the more advanced modes of organization."[30] To ground this precept in the reality of school life we drew from a child's experience in block building and the way in which children of four or five often start with placing blocks in nonfunctional designs or structures, in the manner of younger children. Feedback from the structures that emerge as the result of his exploratory activity, combined with arousal of established conceptual schemata, however, move the older child to become more directed toward building a bridge, a roadway, or a garage. If the teacher does not recognize the value of the more primitive initial play and pressures the child toward more clearly goal-directed and reality-oriented block play from the start, the child is deprived of one of the richest sources for his thinking—the freedom to move from exploratory activity to focused consummation.

Another statement representing the psychodynamic perspective reads: "Growth and maturing involve conflict. The inner life of the growing child is a play of forces between urgent drives and impulses, contradictory impulses within the self, and demanding reality outside the self."[31] Familiar stress situations with young children are less disturbing if we recognize that the maturing eagerness to extend the objects and spheres of affiliation and new belonging collides with fears of loss. That separation can be temporary is still being learned, and it is not easy to learn when cognitive systems are bound to immediate time and given space. The giving up of things, such an important part of the preschool culture of sharing, stirs deep feelings for the young child to whom the beloved object, almost like some body part, belongs profoundly to the self. More than sympathetic support by an adult — namely, understanding of cognitive-affective interdependence within the child — is essential to the teacher role.

For the elementary years I tried a somewhat different technique for conjoining cognitive and effective processes. For each of four goals in a learning-teaching paradigm I described both a preferred instructional method and personality-related processes presumed to be associated with the method. One goal, for example, was to promote cognitive power and intellectual mastery. The illustrations I used referred to two geography lessons, one taught by Lucy Mitchell in 1934,[32] the other by Jerome Bruner in 1959.[33] Both were remarkably similar in setting the goal of stimulating inductive thinking. Mitchell gave children materials to use and a problem to solve: how to place many nations on the land in such a way that they could live beside each other with least friction? With many variables to take care of, the children had to consider alternatives and consult authoritative sources for further information before making their plan. In Bruner's terms the children, in analyzing a similar learning experience, were learning geography as a set of rational acts of induction.

The inference I drew about internal processes (affect) associated with this kind of learning reads:

"The inductive method establishes a relatively prolonged period of not knowing, a kind of groping, in the belief that there will be a "clearing in the forest"; it involves acceptance and willingness to take many steps to achieve a given goal in the knowledge that there is no prior assurance of the relative potency of any one step in the final achievement. In terms of attitudes and generalized patterns of behavior, we see in the qualities of this way of learning the possibility of a long-term influence — toward a general tolerance for ambiguity in life situations, a general attitude that does not see uncertainty as stupidity, and a general expectation that clarity can come at the end of a process as an emergent of experience.[34]

Perhaps that statement helps to clarify, in one sense, what is meant by process-oriented in contrast to product-oriented education. Before tracing the course of theoretical formulations from cognitive theory to cognitive-affective theory and on to the developmental-interaction theory that we at Bank Street consider a minimal basis for educational planning, I want to think my way back to the 1960s.

THE SIXTIES: THE PLACE OF COGNITION IN PROGRAM DESIGNS

The Head Start Approach

It was during the 1960s that the national conscience about the problems of poverty, especially its lifelong disadvantages for children, was roused. A bulletin of Project Head Start describes what a child development program can and should be, its goals, its curriculum, the teacher-child relationship, or, in other words, the whole roster of ingredients of a learning environment.[35] A whole school for a whole child. The clear imagery of what should happen in a school and how, and its crystal clear explanations of "why" do credit to the authors, Jeanette Galambos Stone and Marjorie Janis, who succeed in writing about theoretical foundations of educational practice without falling into a verbal style that Wesley Mitchell used to call "polysyllabic intimidation." Ways of stimulating thinking processes in every part of the daily program are made explicit and amply illustrated. What happened?

Cognitive-Oriented Programs

Though there was a great deal to question about the methodology in broad-scale evaluative studies of Head Start, the predominant finding that Head Start was not solving problems of school retardation ushered in a wave of experimental curricula, spearheaded by psychologists, in which the focus was on the skills needed for children to become adequate achievers in the grades. The wide variation in programs reflected conflicting theories, with behaviorists and cognitive psychologists at opposite poles. I think it is fair to say that, while the techniques differed by which either the "tool subjects" in some programs or the more complex conceptual maturing processes in other programs were stimulated, the early programs were all cognition centered, with minor, if any, interest in the surrounding features of the learning environment or in the interplay of noncognitive experience.

Apart from the problems of theoretical controversy, both as to means and ends, there was and is a broader question to raise. Bernard Spodek put it clearly in a cogent paper entitled, "What Are the Sources of Early Childhood Curriculum?" in which he argued that theories alone are not per se adequate foundation for curriculum building.[36] Instead, they should be recognized as areas of knowledge and human endeavor that should be used as "resources in curriculum building, rather than as [direct] sources." I find myself much in tune with his view and, therefore, skeptical about experimental ventures in which cognitive experiences are extrapolated from the interplay of other developmental processes. I do not see this as the path by which to solve the highly complex problem of cognitive functioning. Thinking needs imaginative, informed nurturing, not head-on training. Edward Zigler has supported and expounded this view.[37]

Varied Follow-Through Programs

The next wave of experimental programs came from the realization that, though gains were made, they were not sustained as the children moved into the primary grades. Nor could it be expected that they would be unless the schools themselves could retain some measure of continuity with the reorientation that had been introduced during the preschool years. The programs in Follow Through represent, once more, the span of conflicting theory and practice about cognition, but I seem to see a change that to me is encouraging. While the cultivation of intellectual competence and power is, as it should be, of great interest and concern, there are more programs in which the interaction of cognitive processes with other experiential processes is a major guideline for curriculum design and emphasis. What is being changed and assessed is a total milieu that is more differentiated, more penetrating, more accessible to analytic study by new techniques than was true of the "whole school" in earlier periods. In place of cognition extrapolated, I seem to see cognition in context. I hope that is not just wishful thinking on my part. David Armington, in some plain speaking for the Education Development Center program, speaks for others, Bank Street included: "We are as concerned with cognitive development as any of the sponsors in the Follow-Through programs. But we resist the idea that cognition can be neatly separated out as just a set of experiences to put children through with the idea of developing certain specified intellectual skills . . . . "[38]

THE DEVELOPMENTAL-INTERACTION APPROACH: BANK STREET COLLEGE OF EDUCATION

This brings my story up to the relatively recent past, the last four or five working years, and I begin by looking at the place of cognition in the current formulation of the theoretical viewpoint that prevails at Bank Street. I have already indicated that we had been moving toward emphasis on cognitive-affective interaction. For many reasons, both practical and theoretical, it became necessary to make a cohesive statement of what has long been called the Bank Street approach. The term "developmental-interaction approach" seems adequate to encompass the adherence to three basic principles. "Developmental" refers to our emphasis on identifiable successive patterns of growth and modes of perceiving and responding that are characterized by increasing differentiation and progressive integration as a function of chronological age. This is recognizable as Wernerian-Piagetian developmental stage theory. The term "interaction" refers, first, to the emphasis on the child's interaction with the environment — adults, other children, the material world — and, second, to the interaction between cognitive and affective spheres of development. The last principle has been expanded to read: "It is a basic tenet of the developmental-interaction approach that the growth of cognitive functions — acquiring and ordering information, judging, reasoning, problem solving, using systems of symbols — cannot be separated from the growth of personal and interpersonal processes — the development of self-esteem and a sense of identity, internalization of impulse control, capacity for autonomous response, relatedness to other people. The interdependence of these developmental processes is the *sine qua non* of the developmental-interaction approach."[39]

The implementation and dissemination of this view takes many forms, whether it is in communication with the profession, in the theoretical framework for research projects, in the graduate training program, or in the Bank Street Follow-Through Program. Communication has been difficult, and it has only been partly successful in the past.

Our Communication Problem

The existence of this problem became uncomfortably real for me at a meeting held in Washington several years ago. In a three-way conversation I was pleased to hear a colleague tell me how our work at Bank Street had served as a foundation for his program design. A third person, joining the conversation, agreed we had done a creditable job over the years, but, he added, "the Bank Street method is a mystique." I did not argue, but my resentment lasted long enough to lead me to initiate another piece of work, small but with a message.

Development of a Tool

In a small pamphlet entitled *Promoting Cognitive Growth*,[40] we tried to present and interpret episodes from classroom life in a simple, schematic form that would clarify the principles governing the teacher's input and mode of interaction with the children, specifically in the area of cognitive functioning.

"To promote the potential for ordering experience through cognitive strategies" appears as one of a list of eight educational goals.[41] In this particular document it was our purpose to make explicit the underlying theoretical framework that governs the teacher's role by relating a series of brief episodes particularly relevant to cognition. It is assumed that an understanding of the framework, printed for easy reference, is part of the internalized competence of the teacher. The part of the framework that refers to cognitive functioning is entitled "An Analysis of the Learning Environment." That part is reproduced below.

A. The components of the learning environment considered essential in order to provide a rich reservoir of varied experience as material for emerging cognitive functioning:
   1. Direct experience with the qualities and relationships of the physical world: sensory experience, large-body action;
   2. Nonsymbolic constructive, manipulative activities with things;
   3. Experience with a variety of modes of nonverbal representation;
   4. Learning the symbol systems: spoken and written language;
   5. Integrating non-present experience conceptually.
B. Categories by which to differentiate the conceptual organization of experience and information:
   1. Identity of objects and persons: e.g., through spoken and written signs, variation in perspective;
   2. Classification and differentiation: e.g., based on perceptual attributes, functions, roles, feelings, processes;

3. Quantifying by different criteria, e.g., size, amount, degree;
4. Orientation in space and time: e.g., near-far, past-present-future, map-thinking;
5. Awareness of transformation processes: e.g., combination, growth, decay, origins, manufacture;
6. Causality: e.g., based on sequence, prediction and outcome, both in physical and interpersonal realm;
7. Formulation of uncertainty and confusion: e.g., by means of informational questions, expression of puzzlement.

In the body of the booklet some thirty episodes of teacher-child interaction are annotated briefly to illustrate the position of the episode within the framework in three ways: the nature of the cognition-related experience being offered the children, the conceptual process being accented by the teacher, and the overlap in the service of the other goals that are part of the total scheme. In other words, as was mentioned earlier, it is possible and useful to enumerate eight distinguishable goals (see note 41), but it cannot be expected that a life episode will be relevant to only *one* of the goals. This requires an awareness of side effects, positive or negative, when any technique is adopted for its effectiveness in reaching a particular goal, which, in this instance, is cognitive advance.

Perhaps only by presenting one or two episodes and the interpretive annotation is it possible to communicate the purpose, which is to make explicit the implicit context of the teacher's way of functioning.

EPISODE:
A girl asks to visit in another room. The teacher tells her she can go tomorrow, tells her the name of the day, writes a note in her presence, and posts the note on the bulletin board. The next day the child forgets, the teacher reminds her, shows her the note, repeats the name of the day, and arranges for the visit.

At the same time that the teacher helps the child to project into the future, she involves her in identifying days by name, thus gaining the means for noting the passing of time.

Furthermore, the note is a means of introducing the child to the functional value of the written word.

Cognitive Competence

The teacher uses the situation for growth instead of denial in a way that enlists the child's motivation in the direction of learning the symbol system for written language. She is offering the means for being oriented and gaining mastery over the passing of time.

Relevance to Other Goals

Impulse control. By being given an alternative to immediate gratification that involves postponement and by experiencing subsequent fulfillment, the child is acquiring the trust that makes it possible to delay gratification.

Interaction. The child sees that the teacher has kept faith with her wish. This introduces a sense of order between intention and fulfillment.[42]

EPISODE:

The reading of a story about firemen stimulates questions: What do firemen do? How does water get into the truck? Where do they get it? The teacher encourages the children to guess and tells them they can check their answers with the firemen. Later she takes them to the firehouse, where they ask their questions.

The teacher's way of reading a story stimulates the raising of questions by the children. She values the experience for its stimulation potential, and she is skillful in receiving questions and still maintaining the story flow. Her goal for the children's participation is active thinking, not uninterrupted, passive attention.

Cognitive Competence

The teacher is stimulating conceptual probing as a prelude to direct experience which will be provided later. A trip to the firehouse will be a way of sorting out the verity of conjecture. She encourages the children to gain control over uncertainty by formulating specific questions.

Relevance to Other Goals

Knowledge. The children are learning a style for finding answers to uncertainty — use what *is* known for conjecture, and then verify by going to the direct source for knowledge.

Self-image. To explore for the answers to questions by guessing, to take a step on one's own as problem solver, to have the ability to hold a question open add to other images of one's self as a learner. Also, asking questions of real firemen enhances the importance of the self-as-learner.[43]

The Problem of Definition and Classification

An educational design with specific goals, a teaching-learning paradigm, and an articulated theoretical rationale can hardly be called a mystique if that term means that the whole thing is an undefined and undefinable piece of lucky intuition. But I changed my interpretation of the word when I saw that there is a chapter in Evans entitled "The Piagetian Mystique."[44] Maybe the word means that those involved know what they are doing, but it is not easy to explain it in a way that others can understand. In that much and more, we share common ground with Constance Kamii and Rheta DeVries.[45] But I find their recent statement a little surprising and, in my opinion, likely to lead to new confusion.[46] They state that their curriculum, in its present version, has much in common with the child development curriculum except that the latter is based on empiricist assumptions about how children learn, its methods are largely intuitive, and it does not appreciate the nature of preoperational intelligence. It is along these dimensions that it is said to differ from a Piagetian curriculum.

In my opinion, the profession would be better served if a term, such as child development curriculum, were not used in so undifferentiated a way that the Distar program and the Bank Street model were both included under it.[47] I do not recognize the Bank Street program as, for example, relying upon or deriving from "largely intuitive" methods. The need is for more assimilation and less juxtaposition.

In the long course of formulating the developmental-interaction approach and, as part of it, the continuous refining of method and rationale for promoting cognitive growth, we have become increasingly aware of the complexity of the implicit decision making that goes on in the teacher's mind. The Bank Street Follow-Through program, which focuses on staff development, is devising new tools and techniques for the analysis of learning transactions in a classroom. The goal is to objectify the decision-making process and render it more communicative.

Looking ahead I would like to see new strength for the child development view as we have conceived it. I would hope that we would find grounds for new thinking in relevant theories of learning and human development without allowing any one theory to dictate the design of the learning environment. I would like to see the skills of continuous curriculum revision and analytic methods of evaluation incorporated imaginatively into the profession of the educator. There is no other way to sustain meaningful consistency between goals, values, techniques, and evaluation. A "whole child" is not enough. It is time to take on the challenge of a whole discipline.

Notes

1. This chapter has been developed from a paper presented at the Symposium on the Bicentennial Child, Washington, D.C., February 1976. It has been kept in the form of an address.

2. Evelyn Weber, *Early Childhood Education: Perspective on Change* (Worthington, Ohio: Charles A. Jones Publishing Co., 1970).

3. Eveline B. Omwake, "Preschool Programs in Historical Perspective," *Interchange* 2 (No. 2, 1971): 27–40.

4. This program was conducted at the City and Country School under the aegis of the Bureau of Educational Experiments. In 1930 it was established as the nursery school division of the Bank Street College of Education. After Harriet Johnson's death in 1934, the nursery school was named for her.

5. Barbara Biber, *Children's Drawings* (New York: Bank Street College of Education, 1962; originally published as *From Lines to Pictures*, 1934).

6. John Dewey, *Democracy and Education* (New York: Macmillan Co., 1916).

7. Harriet M. Johnson, *Children in the Nursery School* (New York: John Day Co., 1928).

8. Charlotte B. Winsor, "Blocks as a Material for Learning through Play—The Contribution of Caroline Pratt," in *The Block Book*, ed. Elizabeth Hirsch (Washington, D.C.: National Association for the Education of Young Children, 1974).

9. Lucy S. Mitchell, *Young Geographers* (New York: John Day Co., 1934; reprinted by Basic Books in 1963).

10. Irma S. Black, *Off to a Good Start* (New York: Harcourt, Brace and Co., 1953).

11. Jean Piaget, *Language and Thought of the Child* (New York: Harcourt Brace, 1926).

12. *Id., The Child's Conception of the World* (New York: Harcourt Brace, 1929).

13. Susan Isaacs, *Intellectual Growth in Young Children* (London: Routledge & Kegan Paul, 1930).

14. *Id., Social Development in Young Children* (London: George Routledge & Sons, 1933).

15. Lawrence K. Frank, "The Fundamental Needs of the Child." *Mental Hygiene* 22 (July 1938): 353–379.

16. Evelyn Beyer, "Let's Look at Montessori," *Journal of Nursery Education* 18 (November 1962): 4–9.

17. Jean Piaget, *The Psychology of Intelligence* (London: Routledge & Kegan Paul, 1950).

18. Ellis D. Evans, *Contemporary Influences in Early Childhood Education*, 2d ed. (New York: Holt, Rinehart and Winston, 1971), 219.

19. John Dewey, *Experience and Education* (New York: Macmillan Co., 1963; original edition published in 1938).

20. Evans, *Contemporary Influences in Early Childhood Education.*

21. Celia S. Lavatelli, "A Piaget-Derived Model for Compensatory Pre-School Education," in *Early Childhood Education Rediscovered*, ed. Joe L. Frost (New York: Holt, Rinehart and Winston, 1968), 530–544.

22. Constance Kamii and Rheta DeVries, "Piaget for Early Education," in *The Preschool in Action*, ed. M. C. Day and R. K. Parker, 2d ed. (Boston: Allyn and Bacon, in press).

23. J. McVicker Hunt, *Intelligence and Experience* (New York: Ronald Press Co., 1961).

24. Lawrence Kohlberg and Rochelle Mayer, "Development as the Aim of Education," *Harvard Educational Review* 42 (November 1972): 449–496.

25. Millie Almy, *Young Children's Thinking* (New York: Teachers College Press, 1966), 137.

26. Howard Gardner, review of Jean Piaget's *The Grasp of Consciousness, New York Times Book Review Section*, August 1, 1976.

27. Robert White, "Motivation Reconsidered: The Concept of Competence," *Psychological Review* 66 (September 1959): 297–333.

28. Richard M. Jones, *Fantasy and Feeling in Education* (New York: New York

University Press, 1969). See especially Chap. 8, "Man: A Course of Study," by Jerome Bruner.

29. Barbara Biber, "Preschool Education," in *Education and the Idea of Mankind*, ed. Robert Ulich (New York: Harcourt, Brace & World, 1964), 88.

30. *Id.* and Margery B. Franklin, "The Relevance of Developmental and Psychodynamic Concepts to the Education of the Preschool Child," *Journal of the American Academy of Child Psychiatry* 6 (No. 1, 1967): 17.

31. *Ibid.*, 19.

32. Mitchell, *Young Geographers*.

33. Jerome S. Bruner, "Learning and Thinking," *Harvard Educational Review* 29 (Summer 1959): 184–192.

34. Barbara Biber, "A Learning-Teaching Paradigm Integrating Intellectual and Affective Processes," in *Behavioral Science Frontiers in Education*, ed. Eli M. Bower and William G. Hollister (New York: John Wiley & Sons, 1967), 141–142.

35. Jeanette Galambos Stone and Marjorie Graham Janis, *Daily Program for a Child Development Center: An Overview*, Publication No. (OHD) 73-1016 (Washington, D.C.: Project Head Start, Bureau of Child and Development Services, 1974).

36. Bernard Spodek, "What Are the Sources of Early Childhood Curriculum?" *Young Children* 26 (October 1970): 48–50.

37. Edward Zigler, "The Environmental Mystique: Training the Intellect versus Development of the Child," *Childhood Education* 46 (May 1970): 402–412.

38. Eleanor Maccoby and Miriam Zellner, *Experiments in Primary Education: Aspects of Project Follow Through* (New York: Harcourt Brace Jovanovich, 1970), 40.

39. Edna Shapiro and Barbara Biber, "The Education of Young Children: A Developmental-Interaction Approach," *Teachers College Record* 74 (September 1972): 61.

40. Barbara Biber, Edna Shapiro, and David Wickens, *Promoting Cognitive Growth: A Developmental-Interaction Point of View* (Washington, D.C.: National Association for the Education of Young Children, 1971).

41. The eight educational goals for the preschool years are listed as : (1) to serve the child's need to make an impact on the environment through direct physical contact and maneuver, (2) to promote the potential for ordering experience through cognitive strategies, (3) to advance the child's functioning knowledge of his environment, (4) to support the play mode of incorporating experience, (5) to help the child internalize impulse control, (6) to meet the child's need to cope with conflicts intrinsic to the stage of development, (7) to facilitate the development of an image of self as a unique and competent person, (8) to help the child establish mutually supporting patterns of interaction.

42. Biber, Shapiro, and Wickens, *Promoting Cognitive Growth*, 37.

43. *Ibid.*, 39.

44. Evans, *Contemporary Influences in Early Childhood*, Chap. 5.

45. Margery B. Franklin and Barbara Biber, "Psychological Perspectives and Early Childhood Education: Same Relations between Theory and Practice," in "Current Topics in Early Childhood Education," Vol. I, ed. Lillian Katz (Hillsdale, N.J.: Lawrence Erlbaum Associates, in press).

46. Kamii and DeVries, "Piaget for Early Education."

47. By correspondence.

5. Perspectives on Bilingual Education

Vera P. John-Steiner and *Ellen Souberman*

Bilingual programs are demanding and complex. It is necessary to identify the children who would benefit from such an educational effort; to choose those models of learning and teaching that will be most effective; to set up a different curriculum; to recruit and train educational personnel; and, most important, to encourage a joint effort on the part of the community and the school system when formulating educational goals and shaping the educational process. When a curriculum chosen by a particular community for its bilingual program is examined, it often becomes apparent that there was no basic decision as to whether the educational model was to maintain the native language while developing skills in the national language or whether the model was transitional, to be used solely for the first few years of schooling. The tension created by the absence of such a decision is inevitably a reflection of the nature of the planning.

WHO SHOULD BE EDUCATED IN BILINGUAL CLASSROOMS?

During the academic year of 1972-73, bilingual programs were funded in twenty-nine states of the United States, as well as in Guam, the Mariana Islands, Puerto Rico, and the Virgin Islands, and twenty-four languages and dialects, including English,[1] were represented. The range of effort appears enormous in terms of languages offered and geographic location, but only 5 percent of the minority children of national origin — those who would logically benefit from bilingual instruction — were participating in such programs.[2] It would appear, then, that the availability of bilingual education falls far short of meeting the need. In addition, many are uncertain about how to assess the nature of the need.

Many parents in non-English-speaking communities doubt the value of native-language instruction for their children. In such situations enrollment into preschool and first-grade bilingual classes has been voluntary, particularly at the inception of a program. Where such efforts have succeeded, parental confidence in the value of bilingual education has grown, and, in turn, there have been efforts to extend bilingual schooling to more classrooms and additional grade levels.

Parental concern regarding the introduction of bilingual education into low-income schools can in part be attributed to the fact that for generations non-English-speaking children have been forced to use only English in the classroom.[3] This has caused many people to reject their native language and to regard competence in English as a basic vehicle for economic success and security in the United States.

There is also concern that bilingual classes will serve as a less blatant form of tracking for children. The practice, particularly in California schools, of placing large numbers of Spanish-speaking children into EMR (educable mentally retarded) classes[4] is well known and well documented. Many parents are understandably suspicious of any programmatic effort to separate children. Any kind of separation has the potential of denying children the right to a meaningful and intellectually rewarding education.

Black and Chicano psychologists and educators have written extensively about testing, particularly about how intelligence tests have been used against children from Third World communities. Verbally loaded tests have generally been shown to reveal greater differences in achievement than performance tests.[5] Robert Williams has shown that, when tests are administered to black children with instructions that approximate their own style of verbal interaction and their idioms, these children perform better than when the same tests are administered using standard instructions.[6] It has also been shown that placing Chicano children in EMR classes in California constituted a particularly blatant misuse of intelligence and achievement tests. Children whose knowledge of English was limited were judged "subnormal" through evaluation instruments that did not tap true intellectual and survival skills.[7]

It has also been shown that there are significant examiner effects on children's tested performances. In a longitudinal study of Puerto Rican children there were stylistic differences between two examiners, both Spanish speaking and well-trained members of the children's ethnic community. Results were consistently higher among those children tested by the examiner who perceived them as friendly, capable, and cooperative.

There is yet another issue relevant to the education of children who are members of minority groups or whose parents have low incomes. More basic than the inappropriate use of tests to classify and categorize children but often completely ignored by educational scholars are the environmental conditions that exist in poor communities and how they affect the full development of intellectual potential among the children that live in them. While bilingual education does offer educational and intellectual advantages to children drawn from non-English-speaking communities, these children and others often face extreme poverty and poor living conditions.

A recent report sponsored by the National Academy of Sciences on the relationship of nutrition to brain development and behavior clearly states: "the weight of evidence seems to indicate that early and severe malnutrition is an important factor in later intellectual development, above and beyond the effects of social-familial influence."[8] The percentage of children from non-English and poor communities who are indeed suffering from malnutrition, birth injuries, or some other medically untreated illness is unknown, but the relative proportion of children thus afflicted is unquestionably higher in poor communities than it is in more affluent ones.[9]

The lack of serious attention paid to environmentally caused (that is, dilapidated housing, lack of medical care, poor nutrition) but biologically mediated damage to poor children has serious ramifications. Comparisons between white and nonwhite and middle-class and lower-class children have been made, and racist conclusions about the relative intellectual potential of each of these groups have been offered.[10] Men like Jensen, Shockley, and Ginsburg have attributed differences in test performances among culturally or linguistically distinct groups of children to fixed, racially linked, genetic variables. Their theories have been disseminated among educators, some of whom accept them as "explanations." In light of the increased popularity of such views, the recently completed and carefully controlled research of Moishe Smilansky in Israel is extremely relevant. Using intelligence tests, Smilansky compared 1,600 children of European and non-European parentage, all of whom were raised in the same environment. Then he compared control children, who lived in communities where resources varied, to the kibbutz-raised children, who, although they had different skin colors and were from different cultural backgrounds, showed no significant differences on intelligence tests.[11] The results of this study are important in terms of generating further understanding of the American situation and countering the explanation offered by psychologists such as Jensen. In both Israel and the United States the lower economic and social position of certain groups was said to result from causes considered difficult to modify by environmental means. In Smilansky's study, however, there is substantial support for the proposition that difference in test scores among ethnic groups is not determined by racial or cultural identity; rather, it is the product of specific environmental conditions that are often related to the standard of living.[12]

Because the impact of the physical environment upon the intellectual development of the children of the poor has been so inadequately explored and is so little understood, there is a widespread belief that most children from low-income backgrounds are less likely to be academically successful than their peers from wealthier homes. This overriding belief governs most school practices, including bilingual programs. Alternatives must be considered, and one is proposed here.

It is recognized that the educational needs of poor children are manifold. In some communities where children speak another language or the children are bilingual, parents and others have chosen to support bilingual education as one means to ensure the survival of their culture and language and to educate their children more effectively. In such communities bilingual instruction probably benefits the children, but an educational solution alone is not sufficient. Any serious attempt to minimize differences in educational opportunities available to children from distinct communities must also improve conditions that support and nurture the capacity to learn. Then it is necessary to evaluate carefully those children who have been deprived to the extent that they may not benefit from large-group instruction, whether it be monolingual or bilingual. For them, other educational solutions are needed, including careful attention to supplementary nutrition, smaller classes, and innovative approaches to learning and teaching.

The overwhelming hope that bilingual education will prove to be an important solution for the implementation of equal educational opportunities cannot help but lead to disappointment and failure without a broader approach to learning. Such an approach would have to include environmental and nutritional, as well as linguistic and cultural, factors that contribute to and shape the effective education of each child.

MODELS OF LEARNING AND TEACHING IN BILINGUAL CLASSROOMS

Contemporary literature on language acquisition stresses the prevalence with which children generate their own syntactic rules based upon the input of the language or languages that they hear. Susan Ervin-Tripp's study of second-language learning in Switzerland is a good example. She describes how children, using their experiences as speakers of one language, develop powerful, heuristic strategies that they can then apply to the acquisition of a second language.[13]

Most instructional programs for young children now attending bilingual schools in the United States consist of structured lessons in the national language and, in some instances, pattern-drill rehearsal and practice in the native language. This approach presents a paradox. The long-range goal of such efforts is to create, in a substantial percentage of the American people, the ability to speak, read, and write in two languages with ease and confidence. Bilingualism could also offer these individuals certain intellectual advantages. Some psychological studies have shown that bilinguals have greater flexibility of thought and a more precise sense of meaning and expression. Such gains could, however, be vitiated by approaches now being used to move toward the stated goals, or, in other words, methods of implementation may seriously interfere with the objectives of bilingual education.

One interpretation of this situation that seems reasonable is that the popularity of instructional methods contrary to those favored by most linguists and psycholinguists as being supportive of the process of language acquisition is an expression of a pervasive fear among those who work with young non-English-speaking pupils. They try to prove that the national language (English) is and should be central to the educational experiences of the children. Perhaps it is this concern that is then translated into a form of instruction where all effort is aimed at the proficient acquisition of English. Structured methods are followed when teaching language to low-income, non-English-speaking children in spite of the fact that other methods have been found to be far more effective in other countries and in middle-class communities.

It is interesting that Ervin-Tripp found that children between four and nine years of age, the age period during which most bilingual programs are currently operating, learn a second language at different rates.[14] Older children utilize more powerful strategies when acquiring a second language. In light of these results, the practice of introducing English to children for whom English is not the dominant language at the beginning of their school careers or in preschool programs may not be the most effective educational strategy. The prevalent educational practice of exposing younger children to prolonged instruction in English may actually have resulted in failure to develop total competence in either the native language or English. The possible consequence of such a policy is that children fail to develop, in either their native or the national language, the full range of language functions described by Michael Halliday.[15] A study on story retelling among kindergarten-age Indian children certainly illustrates the effects of "premature bilingualism."[16]

It would appear that instruction in the second (national) language should be delayed until children have developed a high level of mastery of their native tongue. In many instances this would imply that preschool children should be casually exposed to English, but not expected to produce it.

Educators working with children in bilingual programs must overcome some prejudices when thinking about when to focus upon English in the classroom. They may have been influenced by the literature on low-income children that claims children from poor communities lack skills in abstraction and must be taught by rote and drill methods. This type of approach forms the basis for recommendations made by Arthur Jensen.[17] Jensen describes two types of intelligence and argues that it would be a disservice to black children to teach them using methods that encourage discovery and rule production when their type of intelligence would benefit more by methods that encourage associational learning.

A frequent comparison has been made between the acquisition of French by those who speak English in Canada (as documented by Wallace Lambert and Richard Tucker) and the acquisition of English by non-English-speaking, poor children in the United States.[18] It has been suggested that the greater ease with which Canadian children acquired competency in French, compared with the difficulties that many non-English-speaking, poor children experience when learning to speak English in this country, can be attributed to attitudinal factors. For instance, the Spanish language is held in low esteem in Texas, as is Papago in Arizona. This undoubtedly influences children's attitudes toward learning their native language and could affect their self-confidence when learning languages other than their native tongue.

An additional and related factor is the role of native and ethnic languages in the United States, outside of the schools. Joshua Fishman suggests that "the more a language of instruction is . . . dependent on the school (as a setting for acquisition) and lacks counterparts outside of the school, the less it is rated successful in achieving its goal (of developing competencies in that language among learners)."[19] Most of the twenty-four languages currently used in bilingual classrooms have been maintained in the context of family interaction. There has been severe and continuous opposition to the survival of any language but English on the part of the majority of this society. As a result, these languages were not and are not part of the reality of all domains of living for children born into non-English-speaking communities. The children rarely hear their native language on radio or television; nor does it appear in commercial publications. City children who speak Portuguese, French, or Yiddish seldom see their languages on billboards or street signs.

With these limitations in mind, it is particularly important that the school setting be an effective continuation of the experiences of non-English-speaking children. The supportive approach to learning prevalent among informal and open classrooms appears to be an effective approach to the extension of language needed for these children. (Teachers in these classrooms use opportunities such as baking a cake, setting up a store situation, or developing concepts of number and size and shape that relate to real experiences of the bilingual children in their homes.)

These are but a few illustrations indicating that support of language development for speakers of non-English tongues in America is quite limited outside of the school environment. This must affect the desire of these children to learn their native language and their motivation to learn the national language. The opportunities available to low-income, non-English-speaking children in the United States are more limited than those open to Canadian children or to middle-class American children living abroad.

Studies of language acquisition seem to support the proposition that the full, and hitherto impossible, development of native languages is necessary for the effective intellectual growth of coordinate or fluent bilinguals. Only if pluralism is practiced and adequate resources are made available to meet this goal is the individual child, born into a non-English-speaking community likely to realize his or her potential for acquiring two languages.

Some of the important issues related to the learning-teaching process in bilingual classrooms can be summarized as: the choice of an effective model for learning and development, particularly in the acquisition of a second language; the support of intervention programs that include attention to the health and nutritional status of participants, for example, the model followed in the Head Start child development centers; the reliance on social parameters to develop native and second languages, that is, inclusion of a variety of interpersonal and societal settings; and the importance of timing and appreciation when mastering English, seen in the context of acquiring full competence in both the spoken and written forms of two languages.

CULTURAL DIMENSIONS OF BILINGUAL CLASSROOMS

Relatively little progress has been made in developing bilingual programs effectively rooted in the cultures and the communities of the children they serve. To some extent, the duplication of an existing educational model that is based on mainstream society but has a new bilingual format is unavoidable. The lack of enough trained personnel and the lack of materials for native language instruction are still serious handicaps for the development of bilingual programs. The recently instituted Child Development Associate Programs are aimed at filling these gaps, and they bode well for the future development of pluralistic programs.

It is generally acknowledged that adults in general, and teachers and parents in particular, have difficulty creating methods of teaching and socializing that differ from those by which they were taught and socialized. This contributes to a resistance to innovation in education. Conflict between the needs of generations now in the schools and the methods of teaching and socializing to which they are exposed has been documented over the past two decades by a large literature on alternative education and educational criticism. Most of the earlier literature is, however, based upon the educational needs of middle-class children and educational alternatives developed for them.[20] A parallel literature dealing with effective, culturally rooted educational planning for the economically deprived child is still in the process of being formulated.

One significant aspect of the education of culturally distinct children is the role of educational personnel drawn from non-English-speaking, poor communities. Since the inception of Head Start, aides have been recruited from poor communities to participate in classroom activities. But their role, in most instances,[21] has been limited to offering physical services to the children, disciplining them in their native language, and occasionally providing individual instruction to a child who may be slower in acquiring the subject matter than peers. But seldom have the educational personnel drawn from these communities been equal participants with certified teachers in developing new curricula or cultural-based learning experiences in music, art, or oral history (except for the newly developed Child Development Associate Programs). These fields of instruction, known only to members of a particular community, are absolutely essential if a bilingual experience for children is to be bicultural as well.

The point is made and argued in a recent issue of *The Rican, Journal of Contemporary Puerto Rican Thought*, which is devoted to education, that bilingual programs have to go beyond the language aspect "and recognize that inherent in such programs is a true concern for culture. As such the type of teachers, materials and expected results will be different than if the cultural aspects were ignored. We do not want Puerto Ricans to assimilate into Anglo America. We certainly do not want Spanish to be the tool which accelerates the process of assimilation. Bilingual programs which are good for Puerto Ricans are those which keep us Puerto Ricans, which teach us to be happy with ourselves, keep us healthy and make it possible for us to survive in a hostile

environment. Bilingual programs must also play a crucial role in helping to make the United States safe for diversity."[22]

Some efforts currently underway in teacher training institutions are
aimed at the full development of bilingual-bicultural education. For
example, the Navajo Office of Education, in collaboration with a
number of southwestern universities, is implementing a plan to train
1,000 Navajo teachers in the near future who would serve in classrooms that include primarily Navajo children. Such a massive effort
requires modification of traditional teacher-training practices; it relies heavily upon on-site education and the accrediting of teaching experience on the part of aides and other classroom personnel. Innovative teacher-training programs are becoming more prevalent, but they
are opposed by teachers who are not members of ethnic communities.
The success of such programs would have a serious effect upon the
ethnic composition of teaching staffs. It is unlikely that many teachers
who speak only English will become fluent bilinguals and thus be able
to compete effectively with those who, by experience and upbringing,
are prepared to provide critical resources to bilingual classrooms.
Who shall be hired to teach is a current area of controversy in bilingual education.

One of the least explored parameters of culture relevant to bilingual
education is the pace or rhythm with which culturally and linguistically distinct people communicate with each other and the resultant
need to develop corresponding instructional settings. The creation of
such a setting requires a profound study of the communities into
which bilingual classrooms are placed and greater participation by bilingual individuals raised in those communities who could determine
the most meaningful context of learning, either classroom- or community-based.

The most eloquent spokespeople of bilingual communities have
consistently argued that for each of the culturally relevant areas discussed above (curriculum, teaching and learning methods, teaching
personnel, and instructional settings) it is important to have a community board that has the major responsibility for deciding educational policy and evaluating the progress of bilingual programs. In the
context of creating bilingual programs that are based on a pluralistic
rather than a transitional model, a community board is one means by
which a linguistically and culturally distinct, low-income community
can ensure that its cultural, linguistic, and survival needs will be met
through the education of its children.

THE ROLE OF EVALUATION IN BILINGUAL EDUCATION

The literature on the evaluation of bilingual programs suffers from most of the problems confronting educational research in general. Evaluative approaches to these programs consist of simple, unidimensional tests, which focus on a product of educational intervention, with little consistent regard for the learning processes. Thus, partisans of one or another model of intervention can usually support their particular bias from a welter of often contradictory sets of findings. Nevertheless, funded projects require that some effort at evaluation be included in the plans for innovative educational programs, and the approach to evaluation of bilingual programs is becoming more standardized.

The time frame in which most of these efforts are carried out may result in misconceptions about the effectiveness of bilingual education. Because programs are frequently funded on a year-to-year basis, evaluation takes place during the early stages of a program's development and among children who may be at a period of intellectual growth during which the potential gains of a bilingual program could not yet be demonstrated. In fact, the evaluation results obtained by the Sustained Primary Program for Bilingual Students in the Las Cruces (New Mexico) Public School System illustrate a distinctive performance curve among elementary students in bilingual classrooms.

The program in Las Cruces is well established; it was initiated in 1967 and was described in *Early Childhood Bilingual Education*[23] as having the following characteristics: a pre- and in-service teacher training program developed in cooperation with New Mexico State University and supervised by an imaginative and committed coordinator who knew how to utilize all resources available. Enrollment, as in many other programs, is voluntary; parents can choose to enroll their children in English-only or bilingual classrooms in the same school. But perhaps the most critical feature of the program is that it ranges from kindergarten to sixth grade. These program characteristics distinguish this as one of the strongest Title VII programs initiated in the early days of bilingual education.

Some of the findings of the Las Cruces evaluation, carried out by Douglas Muller show that in the area of academic subjects, such as reading, language, and arithmetic, children in the second and third grades who have been instructed in English surpass the progress made by bilingual children; by the sixth grade, however, bilingual children overtake those instructed in English only. Children educated in bilingual classrooms also did better in academic disciplines as measured by the California Achievement Test, including proficiency in the English language.[24] The bilingually instructed children also maintained a consistent and impressive superiority in performance in Spanish throughout the elementary grades.

The conclusions of this study lend support to the position of those committed to major bilingual efforts. It must be recognized, however, that many factors contributed in the Las Cruces setting toward creating a situation in which children's gains could be effectively measured by standardized tests. Similar findings may not emerge in the absence of one or more of the particularly supportive conditions. The significance of this evaluation lies in the warning that it offers against short-term evaluative efforts. These results, in conjunction with recent reports in psycholinguistic literature, illustrate the lack of a straight-line development in children who are acquiring two languages.[25]

There have been few major efforts at evaluation of Title VII programs. This is no accident. Even researchers deeply committed to an evaluation design find it difficult to compare different classrooms in the same school, not to mention programs in more varied settings, as, for example, between two cities.

The methodological problems that confront the researcher in this field are summarized in a recent paper by Patricia Lee Engle,[26] who states: "The difficulty of separating the effects of the language of initial reading, the language of instruction, the ethnicity of the teacher, and the political sociolinguistic settings of the experiments is evidenced by the fact that few have been successful in isolating any of the factors." She also points out that evaluation studies "differ tremendously in the length of time they allow children before final assessment. There is a serious lack of longitudinal evaluations covering more than a one- or two-year time span."

In addition to evaluation by means of standardized tests, observational methods are used at times by independent evaluators. These observers have frequently reported little correspondence between program objectives stated on paper and the changing realities of bilingual classrooms. A process-oriented evaluation is costly; it is considered "unscientific" by many. But, without it, it is difficult to discover whether an absence of gains in the performance of students in bilingual classrooms is the failure of bilingual education or the failure of the genuine implementation of bilingual education on the part of a particular program.[27]

The continued existence of bilingual programs may indeed be precarious if based solely upon federal funding and viewed from the narrow perspective of short-term evaluations. There are real problems confronting those committed to bilingual education, and the objective of this chapter is to point out some contemporary developments. Among these is the increasing support for multicultural education from state and local governments, as well as from universities. Though some agencies limit their conception of bilingual education to a transitional model, some recent court decisions have suggested a comprehensive and pluralistic approach to bilingual education.[28]

The enactment of Title VII legislation that authorized the spending of federal funds for bilingual programs was significantly dependent upon political activities generated by bilingual communities. Whether such programs become a stable and well-integrated part of the education of all children in states with a multilingual, multicultural heritage depends heavily upon community-parental support and support from the academic community. The distant promise of a fully developed, pluralistic education contains the seeds of educational equality for all children without the loss of individual or cultural diversity and allows the exploration of human learning and growth where the boundaries are still unknown.

Notes

1. *Guide to Title VII ESEA Bilingual Bicultural Projects in the United States, 1972–73* (Austin, Texas: Dissemination Center for Bilingual Bicultural Education).

2. Henry Casso, "Education of Children of the Poor — A Decade Ahead: 'A Chicano Perspective,' " speech delivered at the Invitational Conference on Educating Children of the Poor: 1975–1985. Chicago, April 1973.

3. Although the New Mexico State Constitution requires bilingual instruction in the public schools, this policy has never been enforced.

4. Casso, "Education of Children of the Poor."

5. Alexander Thomas, Margaret E. Hertzig, Irving Dryman and Paulina Fernandez, "Examiner Effect in IQ Testing of Puerto Rican Working-Class Children," in *Annual Progress in Child Psychiatry and Child Development, 1972*, ed. Stella Chess and Alexander Thomas (New York: Brunner/Mazel Publishers, 1972), 149–164.

6. Robert L. Williams, "Stimulus/Response: Scientific Racism and IQ — The Silent Mugging of the Black Community," *Psychology Today* 7 (May 1974): 32–41.

7. Jane R. Mercer, "Sociocultural Factors in Labeling Mental Retardates," *Peabody Journal of Education* 48 (April 1971): 188–203.

8. National Academy of Sciences, Subcommittee on Nutrition, Brain Development, and Behavior of the Committee on International Nutrition Programs, *The Relationship of Nutrition to Brain Development and Behavior* (Washington, D.C.: National Academy of Sciences, 1973), 8.

9. The kind of brain damage we refer to is based on the research summarized by Herbert G. Birch and Joan Dye Gussow in their book, *Disadvantaged Children, Health, Nutrition and School Failure* (New York: Harcourt, Brace and World, 1970). They found that inadequate nourishment may interfere with the full development of a neurophysiological base necessary for the normal growth of visual, auditory, and intellectual processes. This should not be confused with recent claims by some psychologists that poor and minority peoples are suffering from emotional "limbic brain disease" and their subsequent recommendations of psychosurgery as a remedy.

10. A recent analysis of Jensen's research methods and the political context of his work may be found in Stephen Jay Gould, "Racist Arguments and I.Q.," *Natural History* 83 (May 1974): 24–29.

11. Moishe Smilansky, "Kibbutz Study" (Hartford, Conn.: Mediax Press, in press).

12. We refer to the Smilansky study to negate the genetic conclusions offered by researchers such as Jensen and Shockley. It should be clear from our discussion of pluralism, however, that we are not suggesting a monocultural setting for all children. Rather, we are arguing that if each culturally distinct community has the available resources through which they can create a situation where education and individual development is of the highest priority, then full emotional, physical, and intellectual growth will be a natural consequence.

13. Susan M. Ervin-Tripp, "Is Second Language Learning Like the First?" *TESOL Quarterly* 8 (June 1974): 111–136.

14. *Ibid.*

15. Michael A. K. Halliday, *Explorations in the Development of Language* (London: Edward Arnold, 1974).

16. Vera P. John, Vivian Horner, Tomi D. Berney, "Story Retelling: A Study of Sequential Speech in Young Children," in *Basic Studies on Reading*, ed. Harry Levin and Joanna Williams (New York: Basic Books, 1970).

17. Arthur R. Jensen, "How Much Can We Boost IQ and Scholastic Achievement?" *Harvard Educational Review* 39 (Winter 1969).

18. Wallace Lambert and Richard Tucker, *The Bilingual Education of Children* (Rowley, Mass.: Newbury House, 1972).

19. Joshua Fishman, "The Sociology of Bilingual Education (Some Preliminary Effects)," in *Frontiers of Bilingual Education*, ed. Bernard Spolsky and Robert Cooper (Rowley, Mass.: Newbury House, in press).

20. Jonathan Kozol, *Free Schools* (Boston: Bantam Books, 1972).

21. An important exception to the limited role that aides have in most bilingual classrooms is the situation of aides in the Rio Grande Pueblos classrooms. There aides have provided the necessary continuity and stability in schools where Anglo teachers come and go.

22. Eduardo Seda, "Bilingual Education in a Pluralistic Context," *The Rican, Journal of Contemporary Puerto Rican Thought* 1 (May 1974): 19–27.

23. Vera P. John and Vivian M. Horner, *Early Childhood Bilingual Education* (New York: Modern Language Association of America, 1971).

24. Douglas G. Muller, New Mexico State University, Project Director, "Evaluation of the Fifth Year (1972-73) of the Sustained Primary Program for Bilingual Students in the Las Cruces, New Mexico Public School System." Title VII ESEA, Project No. 97-00232-0, Grant No. 410232.

25. Ervin-Tripp, "Is Second-Language Learning Like the First?"

26. Patricia Lee Engle, "The Use of the Vernacular Languages in Education: Revisited," literature review prepared for the Ford Foundation Office of Mexico, Central America, and the Caribbean, University of Illinois at Chicago Circle, May 1973.

27. Lucy Gutierrez, personal communication, doctoral candidate in elementary education and Title VII evaluator, University of New Mexico.

28. *Lau* v. *Nichols*, 414 U.S. 563 (1974).

6. Understanding Infants

J. Ronald Lally

If adults were asked to close their eyes and point to the mind, they would, most likely, point to the head. If infants were asked to do the same thing and they could understand the exercise, they would point, instead, toward the ends of their senses. Infants "think" with the help of the senses, and their thought processes are much less abstract and much less efficient than those of adults. The sensory system of thinking used by infants requires more time, more movement in space, and more energy than the logico-mathematical system used by adults. This qualitative differentiation between infant and adult thought is a key to understanding the infant's view of the world. For the infant, memory is mostly sensation.

Before Helen Keller mastered a common language, the memory of cranking the handle of an ice cream maker was a tingle in the palm of her hand, and that tingle became her memory of ice cream. One can easily see how her "thinking," which was similar to that of an infant, differed from what we think of as normal adult thought. Yet, adult thought has its roots in infancy even though early infant thought looks very different from adult thought.

During the first months of life, the infant begins to modify basic re-flexes and to adopt to the new world outside the womb. Seeing becomes looking, hearing becomes listening, crying becomes signaling, grasping becomes obtaining, and sucking becomes eliciting and searching. The infant gradually changes by adapting to information taken in. The child begins to absorb information, which, in turn, modifies the sensory-motor processes the infant uses to take in information and completes a cycle enabling the infant to take in still more information. Basic sense experiences that transpire early in life are continuously modified, as the child grows, into the abstract super-structures of adult thought.

The infant's major cognitive task, exploration of the world through the senses, provides experiences that move the infant toward the cognitive goals of symbolic thinking. As movement to abstraction is the cognitive goal, movement to objectivity becomes the social-emotional and moral goal. The ability to view self without distortion becomes the second major task of the infant. This task might be called the search for self. Very young infants do not recognize themselves. The feelings associated with getting food, warmth, and bodily comforts are vague. The self is more a sense of what "feels good" and what does not "feel good." A three-month-old infant actively seeks what "feels good." A twelve-month-old infant uses tools to get what "feels good." By the age of twenty months, the child moves to a more specific definition of self that separates self from others by refusing the wishes and commands of others. And it is this ability to separate self from others that is the basis for a later awareness of choice and a still later taking of responsibility for one's choices. The infant starts from a vague feeling of oneness with the rest of the world, then selfishly differentiates "me" from other objects and people in the world.

Remember that, from birth to eighteen months of age, the infant builds a sensory-motor view of the world. At birth the infant uses reflexes to suck, see, hear, cry, and grasp. During the first few months after birth, infants change behavior as a result of experiencing the world and begin to try to satisfy themselves. By four months of age, infants begin to feel their effect on other things. They cause actions that seem likely to continue a display of interesting and pleasurable sights, sounds, tastes, smells, and textures. By eight months of age, the infant shows unquestioned intention and can anticipate future events, for example, mother leaving. Also at this age, the infant is beginning to predict what might happen and can use an object as a tool to gain a desired outcome, for example, pulling a toy to the crib with a ruler.

We find that, after twelve months of age, the infant begins to experiment with objects by using them in novel and unique ways and by combining objects to create new ways of doing things. By eighteen months infants begin to "figure things out in their heads" and begin to build symbols of objects that help to create "new ideas." Evidence of these ideas are actions performed by an infant that have not been practiced or seen before. By twenty months the symbols created form the basis for fantasy and "pretend games," which seem to flourish just before the child's second birthday.

During the first two years an infant also gradually develops a stance from which to use new skills. During the first year of life the infant develops a "rating" of self-worth. A naive confidence or lack of confidence formed during this period originates from interaction with principal others and becomes the basis for interaction with many significant others, nonsignificant others, and for future exploration of the unknown. Along with the increased ability to take in more information, the infant's feelings about the ability to accomplish this feat also develop. This ability to explore the world with ever- expanding tools can be vaguely sensed to be a natural and exciting adventure, a fearful challenge, or a combination of these feelings in degrees that vary between the two extremes. The infant can learn to welcome or reject strangers, to rejoice in newfound independence, or to doubt the ability to handle independence. The child's introduction to independence dictates how future independence will be handled and how newfound fantasy will be used. The process of establishing a sense of trust, of independence, and of initiative is necessary and unavoidable. Erik Erikson warns us not to ignore the need for developmental confrontations that help children build their emotional predictions of what to expect in life.[1]

One of the chief misuses of the schema (the growth of identity by dealing with developmental crises) is a dominant connotation given to the sense of trust, and all the other "positive" senses to be postulated, as *achievements*, secured once and for all at a given stage. A person devoid of the capacity to mistrust would be as unable to live as one without trust.

What the child acquires at a given stage is a certain *ratio* between the positive and the negative which, if the balance is toward the positive, will help him to meet crises with a predisposition toward the sources of vitality. The idea, however, that at any given stage a goodness is achieved which is impervious to all new conflicts within the changes without is a projection on child development of that success-and-possession ideology which so dangerously pervades some of our private and public daydreams.[2]

Much has been written elsewhere about the specifics of infant development[3] that will help in understanding the infant. But to generally understand the work the infant does, one must recognize two "facts." The infant is different from the adult, not just smaller and with less information, but actually different. It is because of point of view and quality of thought processes that the infant does not think and feel the same way an adult thinks and feels. It is necessary, second, to recognize that there is some of the infant in all of us. The egocentrism of infancy is present in the way we think and feel for parts of our adult life, and the bond with the infant is basic because we often act on our own infancy while living chronologically in adulthood.

THE ROLE OF THE PRINCIPAL CARE GIVER

During infancy children cannot provide their own nurture; they can only elicit nurture.[4] An abandoned infant will die.

It is significant that 80 percent of brain growth occurs in the first three years of life, and protein deficiency before birth or during the first three years that is serious enough to stunt physical development also stunts mental development. Hostile physical, biological, and social environments can have a devastating impact on an infant. Nevin Schrimshaw[5] illustrated this point in the figure which appears on the next page.

Physical dependence of the infant on the parent or principal care giver rouses and elicits from most parents the nurture required for infants. In turn, the parent or principal care giver gains satisfaction from watching the infant grow and respond, as well as gaining approval from the family and society-at-large for "being a good parent or care giver."

While providing for the physical needs of the infant, the care giver must also consider the infant's emotional dependence. The world is a strange place to young children. Sometimes it is so strange that it is terrifying. Infants need to feel safe as they explore the world. Young children left in a strange room with unfamiliar toys or unfamiliar adults often retreat, moving as far away from the strange objects or people as they can. Many children become so frightened that they cry or perform simple muscular tasks that have seemed satisfying or safe in the past. When children at the same developmental level are placed in the same room with one of their parents or another familiar person, their responses differ. Most children stay close to their mothers at first, but gradually go out and explore the new world. If frightened by a sudden movement of a toy or a strange noise, they retreat to the familiar person to charge their "security battery" before attempting further exploration. As children get older, they become more secure, moving further from the source of security and staying away longer. People who interact with infants must not only be aware of this, but they must also make themselves available as a source from which infants can set out to explore the world.

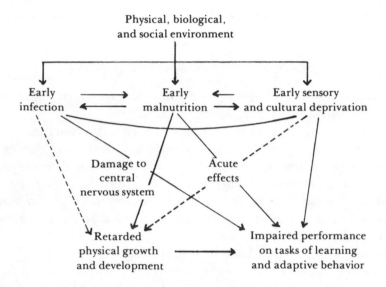

Impaired Learning and Behavior among Underprivileged Populations

Schematic indication of interrelations among environmental factors which may cause physical and mental retardation (Reprinted by permission of Nevin S. Scrimshaw. Originally appeared in the *Saturday Review,* March 16, 1968, from an article entitled, "Infant Malnutrition and Adult Learning.")

Since a child is somewhat immobile at the beginning of life, the parent or principal care giver is almost forced to bring things to the child to experience. It has been established that children expose themselves to new things most readily when around people they trust and that young children take on, in modified form, the values, beliefs, and goals of the parents. Earl Shaefer believes that the early education of a child includes the parents and can be explained by using a four-stage model.[6] The first stage is the development by the parent of positive feelings toward the child. The positive feelings of the parent for the child that are present in the first stage, in turn, bring about the second stage where there are positive feelings in the child for the parent. The third stage is reached when parent and child engage in activity together. That is the point where, both by words and actions, the parent begins to educate the child. The final stage suggests that from this early experience with the parent the child has acquired enough interest, motivation, and skill to begin to function effectively as an individual learner.

Dorothy Huntington, Sally Provence, and Ronald Parker discuss the link between care giver and child somewhat differently:

Directly related to baby's ability to learn is growing self image, his confidence in his own ability to affect the world around him. His sense of competence and effectiveness is built from many sources beginning with his earliest experiences; his expectation that his needs will be filled most of the time, his ability to predict the consequences of his actions with a reasonable degree of certainty, the sense of being able to produce an effect on the animate or inanimate world, and a feeling that someone cares . . . .

When he is very young he will have to begin dealing with feelings of frustration. He will sometimes have to wait for his feeding when he is hungry. He will miss mother when she is out of the room, and not know how to find her. He will want desperately to walk, only to find that he cannot even stand steadily on his feet . . . .

At such times, infants need an adult to help them over the rough spots, to bring solace, and enable them to experience the positive feelings of love and joy. The spark that goes between a laughing baby and a loving adult is beautiful to behold. It lays the groundwork for baby to understand that he or she can effect a response in the world, and communicate with others.

Then, once convinced that the world is a pretty good place, the infant reaches out to it, both literally and figuratively, to explore, discover, and learn more and more about that world. As the infant becomes better able to use each of the senses, the infant's creativity and imagination urge him or her on to further and greater experimentation and learning.

On the other hand, the baby who receives no attention, who is left to feel that no one cares and that the world is a boring place, will not reach out and explore. As a result, he will not learn. For example, by the age of six months a baby, reared in a sterile hospital ward, will refuse to grasp a toy in front of him. If it is placed in his hands, he will drop it.[7]

It should be apparent by now that the principal care giver is crucial. This does not, however, mean that a child's principal care giver must be present throughout infancy. In *"The Good Life" for Infants and Toddlers*, Mary Elizabeth Keister states:

The attitude generally held by pediatricians, psychiatrists and professional social workers, and by informed parents toward the care of babies outside their own homes is to deplore any plan that involves bringing them into a group for all-day care. These attitudes in part have their roots in the now classic "Bowlby report". . . . The conclusions drawn from the studies were (1) that health (and indeed life itself) is threatened by lack of a mother's care in infancy and by even rather short-term experience in the impersonal setting of an institution; (2) that babies above all need to be cared for by their own mothers or by a permanent substitute for her; and (3) that group care per se is detrimental to a baby's growth and development because it cannot possibly involve care by one mothering person.

Hence over the past twenty years there has been the widespread recommendation that if an infant needs day-time care to supplement that given by his mother, the only acceptable substitute would be another mother who could take the baby into her home for the day or a motherly person who could come to the baby's own home to care for him on a rather "permanent" basis.

In more recent years, this view of "maternal deprivation" has been refined by researchers. There has been a recognition that perhaps many of the detrimental effects noted were related to the drabness of the surroundings, lack of toys to stimulate the senses, impersonal caretaking by a constantly changing staff, and impoverished experience with being talked to and played with. The research literature now includes a number of studies of babies who grow up in homes where they experience "multiple mothering," of the effects of maternal employment on children, and at least one study of the physical and mental development of infants in day-care centers. No short-term, intermittent separation from the mother—such as a baby experiences in day care— has thus far demonstrated the damaging consequences seen in "institution" babies.[8]

It seems logical that intermittent separation of infant and parent present an opportunity for either cementing families or reinforcing a kind of abdication of responsibility.[9] Many parents must be away from their child during some of the child's infancy. Economic necessity and psychological need often dictate this separation. Laura Dittmann speaks strongly in defense of care outside the home:

Fear that group care would be harmful was quite natural since there had been a fairly widespread consensus among researchers and practitioners in child development, social work, and the medical profession that babies should remain in the care of their mothers. If for some overwhelming reason this was not possible, it seemed preferable to put the baby into a situation as much like home as possible, with another mother in her home setting. Many states translated this conviction into laws prohibiting the care of infants in groups.

Recently, however, a few pioneering research studies have demonstrated that group care for infants is not harmful if precautions are taken to provide both individualized care by a consistent, nurturing type of person who gives warmth and security to each child *and* intellectual stimulation, avoiding the extremes of bland monotony on one hand, or overstimulation bordering on the chaotic on the other. Careful evaluation was built into these studies and the outcomes are reassuring. Group care not only did not damage the babies, but some children in these well-controlled investigations scored higher in development than did children either in their own homes or family day care.[10]

It began to be clear that group care, *per se*, was not the issue. The *quality* of care, whether it be given in the baby's own home, someone else's home, or in a center, was the fundamental question. Contrary to the artist's conception that all is well when he places the baby on the mother's lap, the assumption can no longer be made that problems related to infant care arise only if the mother herself cannot do the job.[11]

These thoughts lead me to conclude that the principal care giver must assume yet another role crucial to the infant's development — administrator of infant care. Filling this role requires an understanding of what quality care for infants encompasses, the ability to select carefully those who would provide such care when the principal care giver is absent, the assumption of responsibility for the infant's care, and the orchestrating of that care.

QUALITY INFANT CARE

The role of an infant care giver and that of a person who decides how an infant will be cared for are difficult ones. To assist those concerned with infants, Huntington, Provence, and Parker compiled a list of the environmental necessities for providing quality infant care. The complete list, jointly created by twenty-eight persons prominent in the field of education and published by the Office of Child Development, follows.

The environment must supply for the infant:
1. Adequate nourishment from the time of conception onward.
2. Protection from and prompt care of physical disorders and disease; support in overcoming vulnerabilities; physical safety and relative comfort.
3. A relatively small number of adults having continuing, focused, and affectively meaningful relationships with the child; adults who encourage reciprocal interactions.
4. Frequent contacts with adults and other children, contacts that are predominantly gratifying, expressive, and warm.
5. Verbal interaction; a "speaking partner." Sound alone does not stimulate speech development; verbal exchanges do. Free and open verbal communication is essential.
6. The support of an adult who helps the child learn controls — what is permissible and what is not, prohibitions that channel and foster growth; an adult who helps the child learn to become competent and effective himself; an adult who has a

relative sense of competence in handling the child's behavior.

7. Adults who are examples of relative success, who show the child what it is to be proud and have high self-esteem; adults who are models for the child to imitate and with whom he forms positive identifications; adults with a relative degree of satisfaction with themselves and their lives and a relative freedom from depression and a sense of powerlessness.

8. Adults who respect the child as an individual and who respect his family and ethnic identity.

9. Adults who are sensitive to, and respect, each child's different style of development and his uniqueness. Babies are different and all caregiving activities must be organized around an acceptance of that difference in tempo, style, and approach.

10. Relative consistency, regularity and order in the physical and interpersonal situation—regularity of mealtimes, bedtimes, in the arrangement of furniture; stability of adults involved with the child.

11. Variety, flexibility and change in the physical environment, within the structure of continuity.

12. Responses that are dependent on and directly related to, the child's behavior; responses that reward and reinforce rather than responses that are random and unrelated to what the child does.

13. Learning conditions conducive to the acquiring and praticing of skills; opportunities for action, and objects to manipulate, explore, and master; opportunities to utilize emerging skills and support right from the beginning for the baby's use of his own abilities.

14. Protection from overwhelming emotional states such as anxiety and terror; freedom to express feelings and attitudes.

15. A balance of more gratification than frustration; of more rewards and pleasure than pain, failure and frustration.

16. Freedom to be interested, challenged by and curious about what goes on around him.

17. Sensory, affective, and social stimulation appropriate to the child's developmental stage, and individual needs; physical handling to aid in the formation of body image and motor skills; an environment rich enough in appropriate stimuli to serve as a foundation for the development, expansion, and extension of thought processes.

18. Adults who allow and expect a child to contribute to family life and the community, according to his development capacities.[12]

LESSONS ON GIVING CARE

Quality care for infants seems to be based on a precise understanding of the development of the child, combined with an understanding of the way a care giver can best serve this development. The next two parts of this chapter are directed toward providing care givers with some basic information about young children and about how they might best be served.

Individual Development

Age is not the best indication of what to expect from a child. Children develop at different rates and should not be expected, for example, to wait until they are six years old to begin reading or forced to begin reading when they are six years old. To understand the child and how one must react to each, it is necessary to understand the concept of individual development. The process of learning how to read begins in early infancy and is comprised of thousands of little, progressively more difficult steps. Early visual attention to objects, following moving objects, differentiation among shapes, learning that things have names, recognizing and linking objects to a specific label (for example, cat) are all components that help to prepare a child for reading. The child who has not had these and many more experiences will not be able to read. Such activities do not just precede reading; they are part of reading. If they are not part of a person's experience, that person will not read, regardless of age. Different people experience different things at different times; in the same way different people also learn things, such as reading, at different times and rates.

Individual Rights

Neither being young nor being a learner is justification for being denied basic human rights. Neither size nor strength are legitimate reasons to expect someone to do what you say. Such responses as "Because I told you too" and "If you don't, you know what you will get" deny the rights of individuals. Children need to make choices, even though the range is limited by an adult; they need to be counseled in appropriate ways of action; they need to be given explanations for adult action. This kind of behavior encourages the child to accept the choices of others, to make choices, and to be responsible for actions. Adults have rights also, and many care givers allow children to deny them these rights. Respect for the dignity of child and adult must be considered in all interaction between child and care giver.

Individual Freedom

The security talked about earlier should not be construed to mean constant overprotection. Certainly the child's safety is a concern, but there must also be the opportunity to explore. This can be accomplished where a child is allowed freedom of movement in relative safety. This does not mean putting every interesting object either out of sight or out of reach of the child. Expensive things can be moved, but they should be replaced with interesting objects that either cannot be broken or ruined or that can be sacrificed in the interest of providing experience for the child. As children grow older, they need to be allowed to take things apart to see how they operate, to go beyond the boundaries of a chalkboard, to spill some water, to get dirty, and to ask unending questions. This might cause the care giver extra work, but it is important that a child have the chance to do such things.

There is, however, a difference between freedom and confusion. Many "sins" are committed in the name of freedom. Neglect is often called freedom. Carelessness is often called freedom. Extra-long coffee breaks are often called freedom.

Structure

Children should not be overpowered by the complexities and confusion of life. People caring for young children should structure the environment so that some people and things remain familiar. Let the child have a special place to keep things. Do not constantly change spatial arrangements. Remember that the security mentioned earlier can be associated with familiar objects as well as people, and that too much change and too much confusion can create fear rather than anticipation of new experiences. It is important to be consistent.

The "Problem of the Match"

J. McVicker Hunt coined a phrase, "the problem of the match," which, when understood, can be extremely helpful to anyone interacting with young children.[13] The problem is essentially an adult one. In order to solve the problem, the adult interacting with the child needs to provide experiences for the child that are neither too easy nor too difficult. In either case the experiences would prove boring and fail to stimulate. Appropriate experience should match the particular point in development at which the child is functioning. When experience matches development, the child grows.

The reason children do not usually have this problem is because they choose appropriate experiences. They know where they stand in terms of development. Their problems arise when they are afraid to choose appropriate experiences. Those interacting with children should constantly observe the child's actions and put things in the environment that the child needs. This is difficult, but success in matching development creates experiences that help to develop the child's sense of personal worth. It enables him to say: "I accomplished something new. I did a good job."

Imitation

Children identify with and imitate not only their parents, but also many other adults. Children learn language, personal-social relations, the importance of rules, the use of power, and many other lessons by watching adults and trying to duplicate their actions. Adults should be alert to the fact that children learn by watching.

Joint Activities

Children need to learn early in life that they are not alone in the world and that the needs and rights of others must be considered. This can be taught to children in three ways: showing consideration for the needs and rights of the children themselves, allowing children to witness adults considering each other's needs and rights, and expecting children to consider the needs and rights of others.

Different Cultural Backgrounds

It is important to try not to change people's culture in the name of education; rather, one should help children become familiar with many cultures. By meeting different people, eating different foods, singing different songs, learning about different languages, learning how others celebrate holidays, that is, by becoming familiar with the customs of others, children gain multicultural experiences without disturbing their own cultural background or that of their parents. When infants are cared for outside the home, the cultural background of those infants should be reflected in the background of at least some of the people who care for them and in some of the activities in which they engage.

INFANT EDUCATION TECHNIQUES

Throughout the last decade infant education has been marketed and sold to parents and care givers. Perhaps this part of the chapter will help them avoid common pitfalls in rendering quality infant care.

Elaborate Toys and Stimulators

During the first few years of life the infant needs experiences in three basic areas, and equipment found outside the home is unnecessary for growth in those areas. One type of experience, sense experience, requires that the infant should be presented with various objects, usually one at a time, for inspection. Those objects should be "hard," "soft," "sticky," "fuzzy," "large," "small," "heavy," "light," "wet," "dry," "hot," "cold," "bright," "dull," "rough," "smooth," and so forth. None of the objects needs to be purchased. As the infant grows older, he should be presented with objects that require grouping or creative use, or can be used as tools. The child is interested in objects that care givers use and value: keys, shoes, Scotch tape, aluminum foil, cotton, rocks, leaves, soap. Again, it is not necessary to buy anything. The second type of experience involves communication. The child needs attention when trying to communicate both vocally and nonvocally and needs someone to draw his attention. Face-to-face interactions, listening to the sounds of infants, making the sounds of infants, and evoking the sounds of infants help to fill the infant's communication needs. Records and tapes obviously are not necessary to fill this need. Finally, an infant requires secure interpersonal contact with a principal care giver. This type of experience, again, can be supplied without equipment. It appears that such equipment is often of value only to the care giver in that it demonstrates to that person or other important adults that the job of parent is being well done. What an infant needs cannot be bought.

Grading Development

Evaluation and comparison are present throughout life and are not detrimental to development when used wisely. Task mastery is exciting to everyone, and there is a sense of pride in doing something well or earlier than expected. Too much concern for early task mastery and speed of development often leads to vigorous training programs that can be harmful to infants. The fact that an infant can find a doll under a blanket does not mean that the infant has "the concept of object permanence" and can move on to more complex learning. Successful manipulation of one set of materials does not mean that a child "has" a particular thought process. The infant needs experiences with many materials before he really has integrated a particular thought process into his repertoire and can use it as a new tool. Booklets that illustrate examples of developmental progress are often misused by care givers to speed development. Some care givers use only those specific activities illustrated and try to train an infant. Other activities at the same level should be created using different materials and different sense and motor domains. Infants need time and psychological space to practice new skills and to generalize the new skills into attained concepts.

Time for Learning

Remember that the infant learns all day long. Do not set aside thirty minutes a day for infant education and ignore the infant's learning during the rest of the day. Informal learning goes on all day. When carrying a child around the house, going somewhere in the car, going to the store, changing a diaper, feeding the infant or putting him to bed, preparing a meal, or cleaning the house, there are many opportunities for informal give-and-take that help the infant organize the world.

Have Self-confidence

"Trust Yourself" is the title of the first chapter of Benjamin Spock's most useful book, *The Common Sense Book of Baby and Child Care.*[14] This advice deserves special emphasis. As an infant's care giver you know more about that child than any expert possibly could. Trust your own judgment if expert advice seems inappropriate in a particular situation. Anxiety owing to lack of information should not immobilize common sense.

IN PERSPECTIVE

There are now elaborate, annotated compilations that list sources related to infant projects, infant intervention studies, infant curricula, and training materials for infant care givers.[15] Ten years ago, in contrast, most information was transmitted through telephone calls, unpublished reports, conversations at national meetings, or through visiting infant programs. It is the past ten years of experience with infants and infant educators and communication regarding that experience that this chapter attempts to synthesize. While doing research for this chapter, I was struck by a consensus emerging in the field of infant education. This chapter attempts to reflect that consensus. If it does not, I hope that the positions taken will spur a dialogue that will allow professionals in the field to present to parents and care givers in an integrated way the art and wisdom gained from their associations with infants.

Notes

1. Erik H. Erikson, *Identity: Youth and Crisis* (New York: W. W. Norton & Co., 1968).

2. *Ibid.*, 325.

3. Erik H. Erikson, *Childhood and Society* (New York: W. W. Norton & Co., 1950); Jean Piaget, *Six Psychological Studies* (New York: Random House, 1967); T. Berry Brazelton, *Infants and Mothers: Differences in Development,* (New York: Delacorte Press, 1969); Ira J. Gordon, *The Infant Experience* (Columbus, Ohio: Charles E. Merrill Publishing Co., 1975); Nancy Bayley, "Behavioral Correlates of Mental Growth: Birth to Thirty-six Years," *American Psychologist* 23 (January 1968): 1–17; Sally Provence, "The Yale Child Study Center Project," in *Early Child Care: The New Perspectives,* ed. Laura Dittmann (New York: Atherton Press, 1968), 313–325; *Stimulation in Early Infancy,* ed. Anthony Ambrose (New York: Academic Press, 1969).

4. T. Berry Brazelton, "Assessing Reciprocal Interactions between Mothers and Infants," presentation to the Advisory Council to the Center for Clinical Infant Programs, Mental Health Study Center, National Institute of Mental Health, Adelphi, Maryland, July 1975.

5. Nevin S. Scrimshaw, "Infant Malnutrition and Adult Learning," *Saturday Review* 51 (March 1968): 61–66.

6. Earl S. Schaefer, "Need for Early and Continuing Education," paper presented at the meeting of the American Association for the Advancement of Science, Boston, 1969.

7. *Day Care 2: Serving Infants,* eds. Dorothy S. Huntington, Sally Provence, and Ronald K. Parker (Washington, D.C.: U.S. Department of Health, Education, and Welfare, 1971), 13–14.

8. Mary E. Keister, *"The Good Life" for Infants and Toddlers: Group Care of Infants* (Washington, D.C.: National Association for the Education of Young Children, 1970), 8–9.

9. T. Berry Brazelton, "Working with the Family," in *The Infants We Care For,* ed. Laura Dittmann (Washington, D.C.: National Association for the Education of Young Children, 1973), 17–29.

10. Bettye M. Caldwell *et al.,* "Infant Day Care and Attachment," *American Journal of Orthopsychiatry* 40 (April 1970): 397–412; Mary E. Keister, *A Demonstration Project: Group Care of Infants and Toddlers,* final report submitted to the Children's Bureau (Greensboro: University of North Carolina, 1970); Minta M. Saunders and Mary E. Keister, *Family Day Care: Some Observations* (Greensboro: University of North Carolina, 1972); J. Conrad Schwarz, George Krolick, and Robert G. Strickland, "Effects of Early Day Care Experience on Adjustment to a New Environment," *American Journal of Orthopsychiatry* 43 (April 1973): 340–346.

11. Dittman, *The Infants We Care for,* 3.

12. *Day Care 2,* eds. Huntington, Provence, and Parker, 9–10.

13. James McVicker Hunt, *Intelligence and Experience* (New York: Ronald Press, 1961).

14. Benjamin Spock, *The Common Sense Book of Baby and Child Care* (New York: Duell, Sloan & Pearce, 1945).

15. See Alice S. Honig, *Infant Education and Stimulation: A Bibliography (Birth to 3 Years)* (Urbana, Ill.: ERIC Clearinghouse on Early Childhood Education, 1973); Marion Howard, *Group Infant Care Programs: A Survey* (Washington, D.C.: Research Utilization and Information Sharing Project, Cyesis Programs Consortium, George Washington University, 1971); *Day Care 2,* eds. Huntington, Provence, and Parker; Tannis M. Williams, *Infant Care: Abstracts of the Literature* (Washington, D.C.: Consortium on Early Childbearing and Child Rearing, Child Welfare League of America, 1972), supplement.

7. Early Education of the Handicapped: Issues and Alternatives

Merle B. Karnes and *R. Reid Zehrbach*

Perhaps the earliest intervention for children with handicaps can be traced to Germany where, in 1769, a minister by the name of Jean Frederic Oberlin attempted to establish educational programs for children of poverty.[1] In the early part of the twentieth century Maria Montessori, a medical doctor in Rome, devised for slum children educational methods and materials that continue to be used today much as she developed them.[2] In each instance intervention came about because the practitioner observed that children from low-income homes did not develop normally.

Although numerous kindergartens and nursery schools were initiated both in Europe and in America in the late nineteenth and early twentieth centuries, the next major milestone seems to have been the work of Harold Skeels and Howard Dye, who, in the early 1930s, demonstrated the effects of stimulation on the development of thirteen children under three years of age who had been diagnosed as mentally handicapped and moved from an orphanage to an institution for the mentally retarded.[3] One-to-one interaction with older individuals classified as mentally retarded provided intensive stimulation for the young children, and ward attendants provided additional interaction and toys. In an average span of one and a half years these thirteen subjects gained an average of 27.5 IQ points in contrast to a mean loss of 26 points for the comparison group which remained in the orphanage with limited stimulation. A follow-up study revealed that all experimental subjects became self-supporting and functioned as middle-class individuals. Four of the contrast subjects, on the other hand, remained institutionalized, and seven worked at low-level jobs. Their histories revealed poor social adjustment, frequent unemployment, and mental illness. The median scholastic attainment among experimental subjects was twelfth grade; within the contrast group it was less than third grade.

In 1948 Samuel A. Kirk initiated a five-year pioneer research program with mentally retarded children three to six years old.[4] There were two experimental groups. One of the groups lived in a community; the other, in an institution for the mentally retarded. Contrast groups were identified for each setting. The experimental classes were based on a modified traditional approach that incorporated individualized programming, especially in speech and language. Some children were provided with tutors for a portion of each day. For the most part, however, children were taught in small, structured groups with blocks of time for free play. The ratio of certified teachers to children was one to four.

Kirk set about to answer three major research questions:
1. Does preschool training affect the rate of development of mentally retarded children?
2. Do children who manifest an increased rate of growth at the preschool age continue to develop at an accelerated rate when they are older?
3. Are the results similar for children living in different environments—at homes, in foster homes, in institutions?

The findings compared with those of Skeels and Dye. Of the experimental children, 70 percent demonstrated an accelerated rate of development, and follow-up data indicated that these subjects retained their gains over time. Contrast subjects merely maintained or even decreased their previous rates of development. Kirk further reported that the greater the change in the child's environment the greater the acceleration in the rate of growth. Thus, those placed in foster homes and preschools made greater gains than those who remained in institutions and attended preschool. As a result, Kirk maintained that intervention in both home and school settings is essential to promote the optimal development of the retarded preschool child.

In the mid-1960s federal funds triggered a wave of preschool innovations that concentrated on the young disadvantaged child and his
family. Among the researchers who designed center-based programs
for children under five and their families were Caldwell and Richmond; Gray and Klaus; Weikart; Bereiter and Engelmann; Karnes;
and Nimnicht, Meiser, and McAfee.[5] One interesting aspect of the
movement is that each researcher relied on an essentially unique approach: Caldwell adopted a child development approach; Gray used a
cognitively oriented approach that also stressed achievement motivation and the involvement of parents; Weikart relied on Piagetian concepts; Bereiter and Engelmann incorporated pattern drills designed to
help children acquire specific skills and knowledge felt to be essential
for academic success; Karnes used a combined cognitive- and process-
oriented approach that emphasized language development and parent
involvement; Nimnicht's program featured a responsive environment.
In spite of the diverse theoretical bases, these programs had common
characteristics: the subjects were generally from low-income homes
and, with the exception of those in Caldwell's program, they were
from three to five years of age.

The earliest interest was concentrated largely on center-based programs, but interest soon spread, and alternative delivery systems and
even younger populations were included. Home-based programs,
many of which included infants, were developed by Gordon, Schaefer
and Aaronson, Fowler, Kirk, Levenstein, Karnes, and Weikart.[6] It became apparent that there was more than one way to deliver services,
that a number of educational approaches were viable, and that parents would and could become better teachers of their children. In
addition, the overriding hypothesis regarding the importance of early
education was reinforced: the development of young disadvantaged
children could be accelerated if appropriate services were made available. Further, such intervention was highly successful with age groups
younger than had first been considered.

Head Start, a program that represents the most extensive national
endeavor to educate preschool children to date, was initiated in the
summer of 1965, almost concurrent with the onset of the major research on the education of the disadvantaged. The Head Start experience reinforced the belief that the early years are critical ones, especially in the lives of low-income and handicapped children. The
knowledge gained through these activities led leaders in the field to

seek public funds for the development and dissemination of viable preschool models for young handicapped children and resulted in the enactment of the Handicapped Children's Early Education Assistance Act, PL 90-538, in 1968. Since that time more than 175 First Chance projects have been established in almost every state in the Union. The majority concentrate on three- to five-year-old children; more recently, however, the Bureau for the Education of the Handicapped (BEH) has encouraged the development of model programs for handicapped infants. Interest in the development of model programs for handicapped children who are gifted is also emerging.

First Chance programs are customarily given three years to develop their models, replication packages, and strategies for dissemination. At the end of the third year, project administrators are charged with obtaining a funding source to continue the service program. Some projects that have demonstrated outstanding potential for replication have been funded for an additional three years, a stage referred to as Outreach.

The goal of BEH is to provide a program for all young handicapped children by 1980, and each First Chance program is charged with helping to reach this goal. Indeed, a major accomplishment of BEH-funded programs to date has been the promotion of state legislation. Many states currently have laws that provide for the preschool education of handicapped children. Some states provide for such children from birth, while others aid only very young children with sensory handicaps such as deafness or blindness. Many states without legislation for education of the handicapped are now designing such laws to present to legislative bodies; those that provide only for children over three years of age are pressing for service from birth, and those with permissive legislation are seeking mandatory legislation for the education of handicapped children. Although early education for the handicapped has been a viable issue for at least three centuries, only recently has the movement received financial support and roused widespread professional interest. Indeed, the greatest innovations have come within the past ten to fifteen years.

PROGRAM VARIABLES

There is no single approach that will meet the educational needs of every young handicapped child. The problem is diverse and complicated. At least six variables are recognized as being highly significant in selecting an approach to meet the needs of a given situation: the nature of the population to be served, particularly with regard to the range of handicapping conditions; the geographic area to be served, including the density of population within the area; the philosophy of the administration and constituents; the models available for delivering services; the availability of trained staff; and financial resources — federal, state, and local. Since each of these variables obviously places important restrictions on how a child and parent may be approached, it seems clear that the key issues of population identification, choice of delivery system and instructional model, and staffing patterns — including parent involvement and in-service training — must be discussed in greater detail before the components of a sample program can be formulated with any degree of accuracy.

Identification of Eligible Children

Obviously *screening* and *identification* of eligible children are essential before prescriptive programming is possible. It is relatively easy to identify low-incidence handicapped children — the blind, deaf, severely crippled, seriously emotionally disturbed, or markedly mentally retarded — at an early age. Doctors, nurses, teachers, parents, even neighbors are able to detect children who deviate so far from the average few. Parents, on the other hand, are often reluctant to admit that their child is handicapped and are slow to seek professional help. Because of their hesitancy, even their aversion, to recognize a problem apparent to others less emotionally involved, screening techniques must win the confidence of parents and help them become aware of the services available for their child.

Identification of the mildly or moderately handicapped young child presents a quite different and more complex problem. The appearance of the handicapping condition or conditions is sometimes delayed, as in the case of the emotionally disturbed child whose problems do not become identifiable until he has been in a destructive environment long enough to produce markedly inappropriate behavior. Mildly deviant behavior can be subtle, thus difficult to detect through casual observation. Still another complicating factor is that personnel may lack the specialized training needed to identify problems. Even professionals may encourage parents "to give the child a little more time to mature and develop" rather than referring the child to a service that might be capable of intervention and amelioration.

The strategic age for intervention is a related issue. Although research evidence does not conclusively support intervention in infancy, it does support intervention before the age of five. Logic would seem to point to the importance of identification and intervention as soon as possible so that children may be fully served prior to the age of five. Thus it is imperative to identify and provide appropriate programming as soon as possible for the young handicapped child.

There are those who oppose early intervention because they feel a child may be too young to leave the security of his home to participate in an educational program. This makes it necessary to develop service models that allay such fears and concerns, or adapt the program to the home setting, enlisting the services of parents as trained practitioners.

The invasion of family privacy and rights is another such issue. What are the rights and also the responsibilities of states and institutions when asking that parents reveal data about the home and the child during mass screenings in an effort to identify handicapped children, especially when such data also reveal intrafamily behavior that may be in the private domain? Screening procedures that ensure the confidentiality of data and restrict collection to specifically relevant data constitute a step toward eliminating this problem.

The selection of appropriate identification instruments is another difficult task. Differences in ethnic background, in language spoken at home, and in education of parents are all pertinent to the choice of screening materials and the establishment of criteria for further evaluation. A related problem is the question of whether or not paraprofessionals and volunteers can and should be involved in screening and identification. There have been numerous attempts to develop an efficient and effective screening and identification process but there does not appear to have been any comparison of the different approaches on a research basis as yet.

The importance of developing, validating, and implementing mass mandatory screening programs to locate both moderately and severely handicapped children is apparent. Important aspects of any such effort appear to be the further development and refinement of effective screening instruments, the promotion of legislation requiring screening at an early age, the mandatory registration of handicapped children by physicians, the establishment of information programs to enlighten the general public regarding identification of and programming for handicapped children, the development of alternative programs with strong parent components, and the clearer delineation of the rights and responsibilities of parents and agencies.

Delivery Systems

Screening and identification procedures are of little value without an effective means of delivering services that meet the special needs of handicapped children. Four major systems for delivering services to young handicapped children seem to have emerged: home-based; home, followed by center-based; home- and center-based; and center-based. Although common goals and objectives often cut across these categories, there are certain rather clear distinctions that make discussion by category useful and enlightening.

In *home-based* systems professionals or paraprofessionals go directly to the home to teach the young handicapped child or to help his parents learn how to intervene more appropriately. One of the best examples of this system is a First Chance model program serving a large rural area in Portage, Wisconsin. It functions within the public school system and serves handicapped children from the time they are born until they are six years old. The program is financed in part by the Bureau for the Education of the Handicapped. Referrals are made by physicians, local guidance clinics, hospitals, and public school personnel as well as by parents and neighbors. Paraprofessionals and professionals visit each home once a week for a period of one and a half hours. During this visit the progress of the child is assessed, and new activities selected from a curriculum of 380 lessons in the areas of self-help, cognition, socialization, language, and motor skills are demonstrated to the parents. The parents are then encouraged to engage in those activities with their child for fifteen minutes a day during the following week. Behavior modification techniques are also used to promote desired behavior. Recording procedures have been developed in the program that help to evaluate progress in meaningful ways.

Another example of a home-based program is Proyecto Casa located in the Edgewood School District of San Antonio, Texas. This project, another First Chance program, serves Mexican-American children who are from six months to six years old. The teaching staff is composed of high school students trained and supervised by a teacher of the homebound. Pairs of teen-age students visit homes on Mondays, Wednesdays, and Fridays. One student acts as the teacher; the other, as the observer. In-service training occurs on Tuesdays and Thursdays. These students work with the young child and with his parents on activities designed to enhance the child's growth.

Numerous other home-based programs are found throughout the country. Such a system has proved appropriate and effective where there are only a few handicapped children, either because the area is rural or because the number of children requiring special care is small.

In *home-, followed by center-based* systems, intervention typically begins with infants at home. When they reach the age of two or three, however, they then participate in a center-based program. Programs that follow this pattern are found in the public schools of Saginaw, Michigan, and in the Sewall Rehabilitation Center in Denver, Colorado. Still other examples are the Hancock County Preschool Education Program in Sparta, Georgia, and the HELP (Help Ease Learning Problems) Project in DeKalb, Illinois. Early identification and diagnosis and the preparation of both child and parent for entry into the center are characteristic of all of these programs.

In *home- and center-based* systems children are typically served in centers by programs that may rely on a variety of philosophical orientations, but place a major emphasis on parent involvement. One example of such a program is the PEECH Project (Precise Early Education of Children with Handicaps) at the University of Illinois, Champaign-Urbana. Every attempt is made to identify all three-to five-year old children in the county served that have multiple handicaps. The comprehensive identification process (CIP) is used in an attempt to locate and screen *all* children in the county.[7] It is a unique aspect of this program that many mildly to moderately handicapped children who might otherwise go undetected and unserved are identified.

The basic philosophy of the model is to use a structured approach in which small and large groups of children engage in activities based on a game format. The program emphasizes language development, relying on an instructional model derived from the Illinois Test of Psycholinguistic Abilities (ITPA). The GOAL (Game Oriented Activities for Learning) curriculum as adapted provides a base for meeting the needs of the individual children in a classroom setting.[8] In addition, careful attention is paid to the child's cognitive, fine and gross motor, and social-emotional development. Parents are actively involved in a variety of ways,[9] including large- and small-group meetings, individual conferences, classroom observation, classroom teaching, teaching at home, the parent library, the toy-lending library, working with

other parents, the newsletter, speaking at public gatherings, the identification program, the construction of instructional materials, and
policy making. A unique aspect of PEECH is that it represents a joint
effort between a university, an educational service regional office, and
seventeen school districts.

At Chapel Hill, North Carolina, there is another public school project based on a home- and center-based delivery system. Children referred through the schools or by parents are screened by special educators. They are then informally evaluated by a classroom teacher using
the Learning Accomplishment Profile (LAP). Children found to be in
need of services after a three- or four-week conditional placement are
enrolled in the project and follow a classroom curriculum based on
LAP. Parents engage in a variety of activities resembling those described in the PEECH Project above, except that there are specific behavioral objectives that require parent-child interaction. Parents are
also taught how to collect and graph data and how to employ systematic modification procedures. Home- and center-based programs
seem best suited to mildly and moderately handicapped children who
live in areas where travel distances for parents are not prohibitive.

The fourth delivery system, which is *center-based*, requires minimal
home involvement, although parents may visit or work at the center
and they are encouraged to reinforce center procedures at home. The
Seattle Model Preschool Program at the University of Washington is a
good example of center-based delivery. This program serves a variety
of handicapped children, such as the severely handicapped child with
minimal social skills, the Down's syndrome child, and the child whose
hearing, speech, or language is impaired. Children are referred by
agencies, hospital personnel, and pediatricians. The theoretical basis
for the program rests on behavior modification, and individual behavioral objectives are established for each child with the help of developmental guidelines. A curriculum is then designed to meet these objectives. Each child is placed in a classroom program according to the
type of problem and the severity. As the child progresses, he is often
integrated with "normal" children prior to placement in regular classroom programs.

The UNISTAPS Project at Minneapolis, Minnesota, is sponsored
jointly by the public schools, the state, and the university. It serves
hearing-impaired children from birth to the age of six. Children are
referred through the audiology clinic or by a physician. Various pro-

gram options—such as the infant program, the parent-child nursery, a half-day nursery, and full- or half-day kindergartens—are available. Parents are helped to acquire the special skills, as well as to develop the feelings and attitudes, necessary to cope with the child's needs. A unique aspect of this program is that the parents learn at the center, whether through a tutor-counselor during a weekly one-hour session or through participation in preschool classes.

Instructional Models

A major means of differentiating among early education programs for the handicapped is the instructional model used to orient and implement the program. Eleven instructional models have been identified, although it is necessary to point out that some programs rely on more than one. The models can be grouped into five categories. The first has to do with the overall structure of the program; the open-education and structured models are most typical. The second has to do with the assignment of children to classrooms, and mainstreaming or heterogeneous assignment and categorical or homogeneous assignment are the two major dimensions. The third category includes models that rather sharply organize the skills and content of the program. The Piagetian system and systems based on the Illinois Test of Psycholinguistic Abilities (ITPA), on the Structure of the Intellect (SOI), and on developmental guidelines are examples. The fourth category, comprised of models that focus on the ways in which behavior is shaped, includes behavior modification and Reactive Language Therapy. The fifth category focuses on models that emphasize equipment designed to stimulate or promote development.

The first category—*overall program structure*— is represented, on the one hand, by the open-education approach found in the Resurrection Preschool and Parent Cooperative Sheltered Classroom in Alexandria, Virginia. Major emphasis is on providing children with opportunities to learn through selecting activities and interacting with materials according to expressed interests and desires. In this program eight handicapped children are integrated with forty-five other children, while parents serve as paraprofessional classroom aides on a cooperative basis.

Overall program structure may also be based on carefully planned procedures whereby children are organized into large and small groups for activities selected by the teacher. In the course of the day the children can be regrouped according to specific objectives, and may be taught by teachers, paraprofessionals, parents, or volunteers. The curriculum in structured settings is usually based on one or more of the skill models mentioned in the third category. One example of the structured approach is found in the PEECH Project at the University of Illinois in which the curriculum follows the ITPA model as well as developmental guidelines.

The major trend in the *assignment* of children, the second of the categories, is to integrate, that is, to mainstream handicapped children with nonhandicapped ones. Mainstreaming usually takes place in a center- and home-based or center-based program such as the Liberty County Preschool Program in Brittal, Florida, where handicapped and low-income children are provided programs along with children developing normally. Integration can also occur in a homebound setting, as exemplified by the Alpena-Montmorency-Alcona Project. In this instance a handicapped child is placed with a normal child in a day-care home in which the parents are provided special in-service training.

Categorical, that is, homogeneous, placement of children with similar handicaps in the same classroom setting is another method of assigning children. The Langley Porter Neuro-psychiatric Institute in San Francisco, California, serves preschool deaf children with emotional-behavioral problems. The problems of these children can be so severe that they are often excluded from other programs before they reach the age of three.

The procedures for *organizing skill and program content* provides the basis for the third category. The Schaumburg Early Education Center in Schaumburg, Illinois, has developed a program based on Piagetian concepts and screens its candidates according to Piaget's stages of development. The ITPA model is used by teachers in the Preschool and Early Education Project (PEEP) at Mississippi State University, Starksville, to develop activities that identify and remedy deficiencies. The SOI model has been incorporated into the Retrieval and Acceleration of Promising Young Handicapped and Talented Project (RAPYHT) at the University of Illinois. Here young children who are gifted, talented, and handicapped are placed in a structured classroom and follow a curriculum based on the Structure of the Intellect model. Project Memphis at Memphis State University in Tennessee relies on developmental guidelines to determine the child's needs and to devise appropriate curricular activities to meet those needs.

The most familiar model in the fourth category, *instructional models that focus on shaping the behavior of children,* is behavior modification. An example can be found in the Coordinated Early Education Program (CEEP) sponsored by the Eastern Nebraska Community Office of Retardation at Omaha. Another approach is found in the Reactive Language Therapy process, demonstrating the Inclass Reactive Language Therapy Project (INREAL) in Boulder, Colorado. Empathic relationships with the children are emphasized, as well as play therapy and techniques for encouraging language, including self-talk, parallel talk, verbal monitoring, expansion, and modeling.

The fifth and final category focuses on models that emphasize *special equipment* designed to enhance the growth of children. One such project, located at the New York University Medical Center, provides a specially designed playground for physically handicapped children (the Jessie Stanton Developmental Playground). Its special surface configuration helps the child confined to a wheelchair to obtain different perspectives of his environment. A prenursery program for multihandicapped children established by the School of Medicine at the University of California, Los Angeles, has developed a thera-play or fun house that is about twelve feet in diameter and hexagonal in shape. Varied linings of resilient burlap and naugahyde built into the device help the child experience a variety of shapes and textures.

Parent Involvement

Certainly the involvement of parents is paramount in any program for young handicapped children, and a strong parent involvement component is usually an integral part of any program. Nevertheless, some programs approach the parents more directly than others. The Clinch-Powell Education Cooperative at Harrogate, Tennessee, for example, serves handicapped children from culturally disadvantaged Appalachian families. After an initial assessment of the child's needs, the parents are trained to teach activities intended to remedy identified deficiencies. The parents are taught at home by paraprofessionals. Another example of parent involvement is provided by the Agency for Infant Development (AID) Project at Kentfield, California. Parents of children who are blind or partially sighted or who have Down's syndrome or cerebral palsy are helped by individual visits to parents, mother-baby groups, free nursery groups, weekly parent discussion groups, and general parent meetings. These activities and others are used to involve parents. The Technical Assistance to Preschool Programs Project (TAPP) at the University of Wyoming, Laramie, works with parents of children with communicative disorders by bringing parents and children to live on campus for an eight-week session. During this period parents are trained to stimulate the language development of their children and also to learn behavior modification techniques. Following the summer training, project personnel continue to reach the parents through newsletters, providing information to assist parents in working with their children.

Staffing Patterns

Since programs for preschool handicapped are relatively new, considerable ingenuity and flexibility has been shown in developing staffing patterns. There has been a critical shortage of trained personnel — teachers, social workers, psychologists, speech and language specialists, physical and occupational therapists, nurses — in this specialized field, and ways to help personnel acquire needed skills and knowledge have had to be inventive. Often such training is concurrent with actual employment in a preschool program. One method has been to extend the expertise of the limited number of trained personnel through the use of paraprofessionals, volunteers, parents, and even teenagers. Staff need and the increasing awareness of parental rights and responsibilities have given parents important roles in many projects. Professional personnel have often been employed and trained to work specifically with parents using a variety of new or adapted techniques.

An unusual staffing pattern was developed at Peabody College in Nashville, Tennessee, within the Regional Intervention Project (RIP). One or two professionally trained individuals train parents who, in turn, teach other parents how to use positive behavior modification techniques to train their emotionally handicapped children. Almost all project activities, including the training of parents, the gathering of evaluation data, and the dissemination of information to visitors, are conducted by parents.

Staffing patterns also reflect such factors as the magnitude of the screening and identification program, the kinds and severity of handicapping conditions, the age of the children, the delivery system used, the qualifications of existing staff, the availability of new staff, the feasibility and extent of parent involvement, the contribution of other agencies, and the thoroughness of follow-up procedures in terms of overall program evaluation as well as individual assessments.

Training Programs

Preservice training programs are being developed at the graduate and undergraduate levels throughout the country. As states pass laws, either permissive or mandatory, that encourage early educational intervention for handicapped children, an increasing number of universities and colleges are offering such training programs. Indeed, the Bureau for the Education of the Handicapped has funded a few such programs scattered across the nation. There are, however, only a few universities that offer a doctorate in the early education of the handicapped, among them the University of North Carolina at Chapel Hill and the University of Illinois at Champaign-Urbana.

Even when preservice training becomes more readily available, in-service training will remain critical to the professional growth of personnel working in this specialized area, for new knowledge is generated at a rapid rate and preservice training cannot keep pace with the professional needs of innovative programs. It is both right and necessary that in-service training become an integral part of virtually every program in early education for the handicapped.

COMPONENTS OF AN EXEMPLARY PROGRAM

A review of a number of early education programs for the handicapped and of the findings of research-based programs for the disadvantaged reveals certain characteristics that set exemplary programs apart from others.[10] All components are not necessarily present in all programs, but exemplary programs tend to exhibit at least several of them. The order in which these components are discussed here is not intended to suggest their relative importance.

The importance of *early identification* of handicapped children, discussed earlier, cannot be too highly stressed. Maximum success is contingent upon early identification, and the provision of service to handicapped children at the earliest possible age is of the utmost importance.

The *comprehensive screening* of *all* target-age children is essential, for it is only through total screening that mildly and moderately handicapped children can be identified. Any effort to screen all children of a specific age requires positive public relations and helps to ensure the full cooperation of target parents as well as professionals in related agencies. It is no exaggeration to say, at this point, that any program of intervention is only as successful as the identification and screening procedures that preceded it.

When a child appears to fall within the target population, a thorough *diagnostic evaluation* leading to individual programming is the next important and challenging step. Relatively few standardized diagnostic instruments are available. Evaluation requires the assistance of a number of disciplines using a variety of procedures and instruments. Psychologists, social workers, speech and language specialists, physical therapists, nurses, and other specialists must all be oriented toward diagnosing the special needs of young handicapped children, and diagnostic evaluation must lead to decisions regarding placement and programming.

A *positive approach* characterizes exemplary programs, and this approach must extend not only to the handicapped child but also to everyone involved in the program, including parents. To help maintain positive attitudes, plans and procedures must be based on positively stated goals that are realistic, concrete, and understandable to professionals and parents alike.

Still another characteristic is the use of *models for structuring* the program. The complexities of comprehensive programming require a framework that helps to organize the program. One model is not generally sufficient to complete the broad spectrum of program goals, and the most effective programs seem to be those with the most clearly delineated models.

Many handicapped children have problems with language. This means that most programs for handicapped children place a strong emphasis on *language development.*

Since a handicapping condition eventually affects all aspects of development, effective programs attend to the *total development of the child.* If, for example, a child is deaf, helping him to develop communication skills with little or no attention to motor, social, or cognitive development is inadequate programming.

Since handicapped children have complex needs, a *high adult-child ratio* is essential. One adult to every four children is considered minimal, and severely handicapped children may require a one-to-two or a one-to-one ratio.

Careful planning, another characteristic of an exemplary program, includes the establishment of long-range goals, as well as the statement of specific objectives designed to meet those goals for each handicapped child in the program. Careful planning requires the thought-ful reflection of staff members on all available data. Interpretation of the data may be enhanced through careful observations made when not directly involved in working with children.

Then there is the flexible *use of time*. Initial work with a child may require a heavy investment of time, for social relationships must often be established before classroom participation is feasible. When ap-propriate social behavior has been developed, staff and child time must be redirected toward other objectives. Similarly, the develop-ment of self-help skills at one stage of a child's development may be given primary emphasis, but, as he acquires those skills, the emphasis should be directed to cognitive or social development.

To accomplish the goals and objectives of a program, attention must be given to the selection of appropriate *instructional materials*. Materials must be interesting to the child, hold his attention, and mo-tivate him to engage in activities that will enable him to acquire the skills and content essential to his development.

Above all, an exemplary program demonstrates a *humanistic ap-proach* to children, parents, and staff. Each individual is viewed as a human being who deserves respect, consideration, and an opportunity to develop and use his abilities. In an exemplary program the staff ex-hibits real commitment to all aspects of the program. Working with young handicapped children and their parents is demanding; without dedication and enthusiasm, no program can be a superior one.

The complex problems of young handicapped children require multifaceted expertise that is only available through an *interdisciplin-ary approach*. Each specialist must have an opportunity to gather, in-terpret, and present data to members of an intervention team. Only through sharing can information be synthesized and integrated to formulate a total understanding of the child and his family and to de-velop a viable plan.

Preservice training of staff with a heavy emphasis on practical ex-perience is important when launching a new program. An exemplary program can be accomplished with a strong in-service training com-ponent, but excellence can usually be more quickly attained with per-sonnel who have had high-quality preservice training.

Although staff members may have had excellent preservice train-ing, maintenance and improvement of knowledge and skills is essen-tial. Thus, an ongoing *in-service training* program using a variety of methods and techniques should be an integral part of an outstanding program for young handicapped children, and time should be allotted in the daily schedule for such activities.

A strong *parent involvement* component is found in almost all programs of merit. A flexible, many-faceted approach to involving parents was discussed earlier.

Any program of merit must have a comprehensive and efficient *record-keeping* system. Complex problems require the careful collection and recording of data so that both gross and subtle interactions that interfere with the child's learning can be identified and alternate plans devised.

Ongoing *evaluation,* both internal and external, of the program itself distinguishes exemplary ones from those of lesser merit. The continuous gathering and analysis of data, and the application of this information to the improvement of a program is essential in quality programs.

An effective feedback system to keep children, parents, and staff informed is essential in accomplishing goals. Each person involved needs to know in positive terms how he is functioning, and he needs this information as quickly as possible and in terms that are meaningful to him. A feedback system enhances motivation, fosters enthusiasm, and decreases anxiety and useless effort.

The best programs develop effective systems of *communication.* Program staff must be aware of the needs of each child and his family members, and of the contribution that each member of the team can make. Any development that has a bearing on the child's growth concerns the program as a whole.

Strong leadership is essential in an exemplary program. Programs require honest advocates, and leaders must be able to inspire others to contribute fully to the accomplishment of program goals.

Programs for young handicapped children require the full utilization of all *community resources* that can contribute to the development of the handicapped child and his family. Each child may need a variety of services — medical, social, and economic, as well as educational. Only through the complete interaction of all related agencies can an exemplary program be developed and maintained.

While no set blueprint for housing an exemplary program for the handicapped has been developed, there must be *physical facilities* compatible with program goals. Programs that serve orthopedically handicapped children, for example, typically have modifications to accommodate wheelchairs and require special furniture and equipment for physical therapy. Programs with other goals have physical facilities that reflect those goals, such as equipment for the deaf or blind.

Appropriate and sometimes innovative *means of transportation* for children, parents, and even staff are developed in exemplary programs. Buses with special lifts are essential for the orthopedically handicapped, and drivers and bus supervisors trained to handle young handicapped children are also found in quality programs. Careful scheduling of transportation is critical to the smooth functioning of a program.

Placement and follow-up of children into other programs is an essential part of a program of excellence. Established procedures help to make the transition from one level to another and to ensure that needed services are provided. Organized follow-up also provides feedback that helps to improve the existing preschool program for the handicapped.

Effective programs work toward developing and maintaining good *public relations.* All types of media — personal presentations before community groups, television and press releases, brochures, visitation days, the use of volunteers — are used to develop understanding for the program and gain support for the program from the community-at-large.

Administrative support is crucial in promoting and maintaining a high level of operation. This support includes reinforcement not only from immediate supervisors but also from higher levels of administration. People working in a program for young handicapped children need to be aware that the administration endorses the program and appreciates the efforts of everyone involved. In the last analysis, the administration is largely responsible for ensuring that all components of an exemplary program are present. Where this is the case, staff morale is almost invariably high.

Notes

1. Frances D. Horowitz and Lucile Y. Paden, "The Effectiveness of Environmental Intervention Programs," in *Review of Child Development Research.* Vol. III, *Child Development and Social Policy,* ed. Bettye M. Caldwell and Henry Riccuiti (Chicago: University of Chicago Press, 1973), 331–402.

2. Maria Montessori, *The Montessori Method* (New York: Frederich A. Stokes, 1912).

3. Harold M. Skeels and Howard B. Dye, "A Study of the Effects of Differential Stimulation on Mentally Retarded Children," *Proceedings of the Annual Convention of the American Association of Mental Deficiency* 44 (1939): 114–136; Harold M. Skeels, *Adult Status of Children with Contrasting Early Life Experiences: A Follow-*

up Study, Monograph No. 105, *Monographs of the Society for Research in Child Development* 31 (No. 3, 1966).

4. Samuel A. Kirk, *Early Education of the Mentally Retarded* (Urbana, Ill.: University of Illinois Press, 1958).

5. Bettye M. Caldwell and Julius B. Richmond, "The Children's Center in Syracuse, New York," in *Early Child Care: The New Perspectives,* ed. Laura L. Dittmann (New York: Atherton Press, 1968), 326–358; Rupert A. Klaus and Susan W. Gray, *The Early Training Project for Disadvantaged Children: A Report after Five Years,* Monograph No. 120, *Monographs of the Society for Research in Child Development* 33, (No. 4, 1968): 1–66; David P. Weikart, "Preschool Programs: Preliminary Findings," *Journal of Special Education* 1 (Winter 1967): 163–181; Carl Bereiter and Siegfried Engelmann, *Teaching Disadvantaged Children in the Preschool* (Englewood Cliffs, N.J.: Prentice-Hall, Inc., 1966); Merle B. Karnes *et al.,* "An Approach for Working with Mothers of Disadvantaged Preschool Children," *Merrill-Palmer Quarterly* 14 (April 1968): 174–184; Glen Nimnicht, John M. Meier, and Oralie McAfee, "Interim Report: Research on the New Nursery School," Colorado State College, Greeley, Colorado, December 1967.

6. Ira J. Gordon, "Early Child Stimulation through Parent Education," final report to the Children's Bureau, U.S. Department of Health, Education, and Welfare, PHS-R-306 (01) (Gainesville, Fla.: Institute for Development of Human Resources, College of Education, University of Florida, June 30, 1969); Earl S. Schaefer and May Aaronson, "Infant Education Research Project: Implementation and Implications of a Home Tutoring Program," in *The Preschool in Action,* ed. Ronald K. Parker (Boston: Allyn & Bacon, 1972), 410–430; William A. Fowler, "A Developmental Learning Approach to Infant Care in a Group Setting," *Merrill-Palmer Quarterly* 18 (April 1972): 145–175; Kirk, *Early Education of the Mentally Retarded;* Phyllis Levenstein, "Verbal Interaction Project: Aiding Cognitive Growth in Disadvantaged Preschoolers through the Mother-Child Home Program, July 1, 1967—August 31, 1970," final report of Child Welfare, Research and Demonstration Project R-300 to the Children's Bureau, Office of Child Development, U.S. Department of Health, Education, and Welfare, February 1971; Merle B. Karnes, "Evaluation and Implications of Research with Young Handicapped and Low-income Children," in *Compensatory Education for Children, Ages 2 to 8,* ed. Julian C. Stanley (Baltimore, Md.: Johns Hopkins University Press, 1973), 109–144; David P. Weikart, "Ypsilanti-Carnegie Infant Education Project," Progress Report (Ypsilanti, Mich.: Department of Research and Development, Ypsilanti Public Schools, September 1969).

7. R. Reid Zehrbach, "Determining a Preschool Handicapped Population," *Exceptional Children* 42 (October 1975): 76–83; *id., CIP: Comprehensive Identification Process,* a screening test for 2½- to 5½-year-old handicapped children (Bensenville, Ill.: Scholastic Testing Service, 1975).

8. Merle B. Karnes, *GOAL: Language Development* (Springfield, Mass.: Milton Bradley Co., 1972; *id., GOAL: Mathematical Concepts* (Springfield, Mass.: Milton Bradley Co., 1973).

9. Merle B. Karnes and R. Reid Zehrbach, "Flexibility in Getting Parents Involved in the School," *Teaching Exceptional Children* 5 (Fall 1972): 6–19; *id.,* "Curriculum

and Methods in Early Childhood Special Education: One Approach," *Focus on Exceptional Children* 5 (April 1973): 1-12.

10. Merle B. Karnes, "Education of Preschool Age Handicapped Children," in *Special Education—Needs—Costs—Methods of Financing: Report of a Study,* comp. W. P. McClure, R. A. Burnham, and R. A. Henderson, for the Illinois School Problems Commission, Illinois Office of Education (Urbana, Ill.: Bureau of Educational Research, College of Education, University of Illinois, May 1975), 73-87.

8. Curriculum Construction in Early Childhood Education

Bernard Spodek

While the process of educating young children is probably as old as the human race, the actual establishment of schools specifically designed for young children is a relatively recent phenomenon, found only in the last century and a half. The history of these schools is characterized by both continuity and discontinuity. Modern ideas have developed and replaced older ideas, while at the same time vestiges of the old continue to intrude upon the new. Although the last fifteen years can be characterized as the most active period in curriculum construction in the history of early childhood education, most program practices observed in nursery schools, kindergartens, and day-care centers have been with us for quite a while.

The continuity present in early childhood education can be seen in the persistent concern of programs for one of two types of goals for young children. One concern has been for the support or stimulation of growth or development. The other has been for achieving specific learnings. What has changed over time or from program to program is how growth has been conceptualized or what particular learnings were considered important.

Marvin Lazerson has suggested that three themes have dominated the history of early childhood education in the United States.[1] The

116

first one relates to the uses of early schooling to achieve social reform. In early times kindergartens were established by philanthropic institutions to provide services to children of immigrant or slum families. More recently federal thrusts such as the Head Start and Follow-Through programs, originally designed as part of the "war on poverty," were seen as ways of compensating disadvantaged children for their backgrounds and helping them join the mainstream of American life.

Lazerson's second theme relates to the uniqueness and importance of childhood. It is concepts of developmental stages that have led to a separation of childhood from adulthood. In some instances childhood has been viewed as a period that has limited impact on the total development of the individual and, therefore, it deserves little attention. Others have seen the early childhood stage as the period that has the greatest impact on the total development of the individual. One example of this point of view is Benjamin Bloom's notion that half of the development of an individual's intelligence can be accounted for in the first four years of life.[2]

The third theme relates to the impact of early childhood education on the school. Making early childhood programs a part of public education has affected the rest of the educational establishment. This impact, along with the impact of the existing school on the early childhood program, has been a concern of educators since the beginning of the twentieth century. Benjamin Gregory, for example, discussed ways in which Froebelian practices could be carried into the elementary school.[3]

Each of the three themes identified by Lazerson has been manifest not only in the developing of educational programs for young children, but in the content of the programs offered. Curriculum conceptions have been created for early childhood education that differ from those of other parts of the educational enterprise. The rationale behind programs designed for early childhood education has also proved unique in the broader field of education. Prior conceptions of early childhood curriculum construction do provide a context in which to view more contemporary approaches.

HISTORICAL CONCEPTIONS OF CURRICULUM

The earliest conception of a curriculum designed especially for young children can be found in the work of Friedrich Froebel. The program generated by Froebel was an outgrowth of his views on the nature of childhood and the nature of the world. Froebel viewed development as occurring in stages, with later stages dependent upon the fulfillment of earlier ones. In the early stages, knowledge was thought to result from actions of the child. This idea resembles the "operations" found in Piagetian theory. Education was viewed as originating in actions, with living, doing, and knowing seen as connected processes. According to Froebel, insight and knowledge developed hand in hand with the creative processes, a conception still held by many contemporary early childhood educators.

To Froebel the world was a living work and a manifestation of God. It contained a universal order that was all-pervading, self-cognizant, and everlasting. Since man's responsibility was to understand that order and man's role within it, Froebel identified the goal of education as being an understanding of the unity of man, God, and nature. Froebel used the metaphor of the garden to characterize an education that should follow the nature of the child but could not mold or impose upon it. He elaborated a curriculum using symbolic activities that would allow the child's potential to unfold as he was presented with representations of the basic conception of the order of the world according to Froebel. Froebel's use of the "gifts" as curriculum materials illustrates his concern for symbolic learning. The first gift, a set of worsted balls, symbolized the concept of the unity of God, man, and nature. The second gift, consisting of a ball, a cube, and a cylinder, symbolized unity, diversity, and the mediation of opposites.[4]

Froebel's kindergarten program was disseminated throughout the world. It had great impact on the infant school curriculum in England as it moved toward greater informality and became more child centered. It also influenced the modern progressive American kindergarten, although both the ends and means of kindergarten education have been modified in the United States and England.[5] Both the Montessori school and the nursery school reflect Froebel's ideas.

From a historical point of view the next major conception of early childhood that continues to have impact upon the current curriculum was developed by Maria Montessori. While Montessori's view of human development resembled that of Froebel, her concept of educational activities appropriate for young children was quite different.

For Froebel, the symbolic meanings of materials and activities were important. For Montessori, the physical attributes of educational materials and the skills to be attained from their proper use assumed more importance. Montessori was concerned with having young children increase their sensitivity to impressions and improve the uses that they made of these sensory impressions through information-processing techniques. The skills needed in practical life situations and in basic academic areas were also important. To this end Montessori provided materials that differed in visual, auditory, tactile, baric, and thermal qualities. Children were taught to discriminate between different intensities or pitches of sounds made by objects enclosed in a box or between different colors, sizes, and weights of materials. They were also provided with precise ways of opening a door, dusting their classroom, and pouring a glass of water.[6] While Froebel's program was supportive of development in general, Montessori's was essentially instructional, although the instruction provided was mostly of an indirect kind. The use of a prepared environment, with self-correcting materials that were used in specified sequences of activities, predated the programs of individualized and programmed instruction found in schools today. The goal of each set of activities was clearly specified, and equipment and activities were developed to aid in the achievement of that goal, whether the goal was to learn to distinguish colors or sizes, to wash one's hands, to add, or to write the letters of the alphabet.

The third historical movement in curriculum construction for early childhood was the creation of the nursery school. This paralleled a fourth movement, the reformation of the kindergarten and the creation of the progressive kindergarten program that is with us today. The nursery school developed prior to World War I was designed to serve as an avenue for social reform. If it did not diminish the inequities of English society, the nursery school could at least alleviate some of the consequences of those inequities for urban slum children. The social purposes of the nursery school seem to have been forgotten in its continued development as the schools had to depend upon tuition payments from their students to survive. What was originally intended as a salve for the poor became a comfort primarily for the affluent.

The nursery school, much as the Froebelian kindergarten, was viewed as supporting development. Activities, however, were intended less to represent higher-order relationships between man, God, and the universe and more to help children cope with their immediate life situations. Understanding the world around them was stressed as an important element of education for these children, as was the increased development of the imagination. Nurturance was a concept underlying the educational and social goals of the school. Although the program contained activities to teach self-caring skills and perceptual discrimination, less specific activities were emphasized, and the focus of the program was on play, on expressive activities, and on an avoidance of premature imposition.[7]

The same emphases were to be found in the reform kindergarten. Although a behavioral emphasis characterized some curriculum construction of the 1920s, the reform kindergarten manifested a concern for free play, for projects, and for expressive activities based upon assumptions regarding the young child's use of play as a vehicle for learning at this stage of development.[8]

It is interesting to note that the two basic thrusts in early childhood curriculum construction that have influenced programs of early childhood education to this day, those of Froebel and Montessori, occurred independent of and prior to the establishment of the child study movement. This movement to study children scientifically had a major impact on later curriculum construction, especially in the nursery school and the progressive kindergarten, and continues to be an important resource for curriculum construction today. Various approaches to child study or child development theory used to suggest refined procedures or to provide a rationale for existing practices did not change in any major way the two thrusts, concern for growth and concern for learning, already established in the field.

EARLY EDUCATION AND CHILD DEVELOPMENT

The establishment of the field of child study, which later became the field of child development, paralleled a shift in the field of psychology from a view that human beings can best be studied through introspection or speculation to a view that human beings can best be studied through observation. It was this basic shift in orientation that aligned psychology with the empirical sciences, rather than with philosophy. By the mid-nineteenth century, observations and biographies of children, such as those by Charles Darwin and Wilhelm Preyer, set the tone of study. Later, more rigorous methods of child observation and testing were developed by G. Stanley Hall and Alfred Binet.

According to Bruce Gardner, four major streams of child study have contributed to the establishment of contemporary child development theory: behaviorist, normative-descriptive, field theory, and psychoanalytic.[9] Up to the mid-1960s the normative-descriptive and the psychoanalytic approaches probably had the greatest influence on curriculum development for early childhood. These views were most consistent with the thought of Froebel and Margaret Macmillan.

Sigmund Freud, whose concern for personality development provided the cornerstone of psychoanalytic theory, viewed child development as a series of psychosexual stages leading to maturity. Problems arising at any stage of development could thwart the achievement of maturity, and immature acts could be controlled in the adult through unconscious mechanisms. The view of Freud and his followers led early childhood specialists to view education as an emotional prophylaxis, limiting the major frustrations of childhood and providing for the catharsis of difficult experience. The teacher's role, as a supporter of development and as a provider of activities for the expression of emotions through dramatic play, craft activities, or some other expressive activity, was consistent with the ideas of both Froebel and Freud.

Arnold Gesell and his colleagues are probably the best-known of the normative-descriptive child development specialists. This approach is concerned with providing a description of normal processes of development for children. Samples of motor, social, intellectual, and language behavior collected through careful observations were organized according to the ages of children observed. The masses of information were then collated into a set of averages and ranges of behavior, organized by age, which were established as "norms." Using the norms, one could plot the rate of growth for all children as well as identify the relationship of a single child's development to a total population of children of comparable age, thus identifying slow as well as fast developers.

The conception of the nature of development underlying the normative-descriptive approach was similar to that of Froebel's view of "unfolding." It was believed that, while one could nurture or thwart development, in the final analysis the basis for the total development of the child was inherent in his physical makeup. The role of early education conceived from this point of view was to follow and support, rather than determine, development. Little else but frustration would result from pushing a child beyond his capability.

During the first half of the twentieth century most early childhood programs were consistent with a normative-descriptive or maturationist point of view. No specific learning tasks were identified as educational goals. Rather, early childhood education was generally seen as supportive of development. Educationists were less concerned with the effects of environment on the young child or with what the child learned than with providing as good a set of environmental conditions as possible in support of development. While what a child learned was important, there was a fear of imposing specific learning in the belief that a loosely constructed, supportive educational environment would allow the child to set his own pace and find his own way toward whatever achievement goals were desirable.

Given this point of view, the focus of the nursery school and of the kindergarten was on providing appropriate experiences and activities for children, and it was the quality of those activities, rather than the resultant learning outcomes, that formed the basis for curriculum evaluation. Thus, a conception of curriculum was introduced into the field that was self-validating. Since development was a long-term process, it was considered foolish to focus on short-term outcomes, for there was no evidence that the achievement of any short-term goals would actually lead to an improvement in the longer-term goal of optimum development. This attitude was reinforced by the idea that long-term assessment was fruitless because many experiences coming after early education could distort the outcome and account for what the adult would ultimately become.

Lawrence Kohlberg and Rochelle Mayer, in a recent article, identified three thrusts of education: a "romantic" thrust, a "cultural transmission" thrust, and a "progressive" thrust.[10] The conception of development as a process of unfolding underlies the romantic thrust. Education based on this conception is seen as essentially a support for development. The cultural transmission thrust is concerned with transferring elements of culture from an older to a younger generation, and there is little concern for developmental theory. The third thrust, labeled progressive, views development as occurring through the interaction of the individual with his environment and with the individual's actions on his environment—essentially, the individual creates his own development. Given this tripartite view of education, it would appear that the mainstream of early childhood education during the first half of the twentieth century was primarily affected by the romantic thrust. As shown earlier, however, elements of the cultural transmission thrust can be found in the "conduct curriculum" of the progressive kindergarten. During this period the focus of early childhood classes was on activities. Many of the activities suggested as appropriate for young children resembled the activities found in the original Froebelian curriculum, but they were modified to accord with research findings or to conform more closely to American habits. Such activities included paper folding, weaving, and cutting; drawing pictures; singing; and playing games.

This Froebelian view of development as unfolding led the nursery school educator to view curriculum as being derived from the observations of children, much as Froebel had done a century earlier. Curriculum construction, according to Harriet Johnson, one of the pioneers of the American nursery school movement, required "an ordered analysis of observed behaviors; the outlining of stages and phases in development; and the conception of certain interests and impulses dominant in early childhood. It must also assume a logical relationship between the trends in behavior and the educational processes . . . . "[11] Interestingly, while Johnson saw the nursery school curriculum as following the interests of children, it was not expected that those interests would be followed blindly. Rather, the nursery school teacher, in constructing her curriculum must "know the attitudes, interests and capacities she believed it desirable to foster, why she considers them important and by what methods she proposes to further their development among children in her care."[12] The development of traits and attitudes often not clearly identifiable in observed behavior, rather than skills or specified performance, were seen as the goals of early childhood education. Values, it seems, played an important part in deciding which traits and attitudes should be fostered in nursery school and which should be discarded or suppressed. Whether these values should be those of the larger society, those of the children's parents, or those of a particular school is not evident in Johnson's writing. Nor is there any analysis of the worth of some values or any criteria for selecting appropriate ones.

One essential belief that resulted from the nursery school point of view was the importance of "growth." Growth was seen as "development in power and control; control of body, a growing power to deal with the environment and to understand their relationship to it, with a resulting harmony in functioning."[13] Toward this end teachers were to become students of child behavior, observing closely to identify universal impulses and stages. What they learned from observation could be fed back into curriculum construction in their classrooms.

For most early childhood educators the idea of growth as an aim of education, conceived in a framework of maturational development, led to a program at the nursery school and kindergarten levels that was protective at best. As kindergartens became a part of the public elementary schools, however, they not only influenced the rest of the school, as Lazerson suggests, but they were heavily influenced by it. The imposition of the primary curriculum led to modification of the kindergarten to include activities that would prepare children for later specific instruction as well as help them develop. This "readiness" view of the kindergarten was actively opposed by many early childhood educators. Roma Gans, Millie Almy, and Celia Stendler characterize this readiness view of kindergarten as the "3Rs Curriculum":

The 3Rs approach has not only prevailed in the primary grades, but it has reached down into the five-year-old kindergarten. Counting, some writing, and reading readiness activities chiefly in the form of workbook exercises, have been typical experiences in kindergartens where this curriculum has been in operation. Under such a setup the kindergarten is seen as a year of settling down for children, of adjusting to sitting still and following directions, so that they will be better prepared for a more rigorous attack on the 3Rs during first grade.[14]

This argument against including academic learning in the kindergarten curriculum was based on a view of its inefficiency, since it did not take into account the "psychological arrangement" of knowledge; on a belief that it ignored the interests and activities of the learner; and on its lack of intellectual challenge.[15]

This, then, was the state of early childhood education until the era of the 1960s — a concern for children's natural development, a fear of too much imposition from the elementary grades, and a view that educational practice could develop from observations of children, with early education to support that development. In the 1960s a number of influences converged that had a major impact, if not on the practice of early childhood education, at least on the ways in which curriculum practice was justified. These changes resulted both from changes in developmental theory, changes in the relationship between such theory and curriculum development, and changes in social priorities that placed new demands on the outcomes of early schooling.

NEWER CURRICULUM CONCEPTIONS

During the 1960s there was heightened concern over obtaining social justice for poor people and for members of minority groups. It was believed that under the proper conditions all persons could join in the mainstream of an affluent society. One of the most visible differences between the affluent and the poor was the level of school achievement. One goal of the war on poverty was to help the poor move into the middle class. It was believed that, by improving school achievement among the poor, there would be a parallel rise in social mobility. Thus it was that intellectual and academic achievement came to be seen as a basis for affluence, and it led to a search for ways to improve the academic performance of "disadvantaged" children. There were programs to bring dropouts back into school, to make poorer persons more aware of educational opportunities, and to increase motivation for achieving academic success in the secondary schools. One of the more attractive approaches was the establishment of educational programs for children prior to their admission to the regular elementary school. In keeping with Lazerson's analysis of themes, early childhood educators again responded to the call to use early schooling to achieve social reform.

Since "disadvantaged" children, as they came to be called, were significantly different in their family and cultural backgrounds from affluent children and since they were less successful in their culture, a concept of cultural deficit was postulated. Somehow the backgrounds of middle-class children provided them with prerequisites for school success that were absent in lower-class children. If the deficit could be eliminated prior to the child's initial enrollment in school, the probability of continued academic success would increase, thereby making a major impact on the future lives and careers of the young children.

There was support for the idea that preschool programs of compensatory education had an impact on disadvantaged children. The belief that there was a "hidden curriculum" in middle-class, child-rearing practices[16] that was absent in lower-class, child-rearing practices, as well as the recognition that there were different language codes among the advantaged and the disadvantaged[17] provided support for new programs of compensatory education. There was also support for providing these programs at the earliest possible time in the life of a child.

At about the same time as concern was growing over the education of the disadvantaged, cognitive development was receiving greater attention. During the late 1950s American psychologists and educators became aware of the work of Jean Piaget, which had been accumulating for decades. Piaget conceptualized children's cognitive development as a series of stages, with achievement at later stages dependent upon successful progress through earlier ones. The early experiences of the child were seen as having a significant impact on total intellectual development, even though direct instruction was not considered to be effective in moving children through the stages. J. M. Hunt, in his classic formulation, *Intelligence and Experience*, brought together a wealth of data from many sources supporting the idea that the experience of the organism, especially that occurring during early childhood, had a major impact on the developing intellect.[18] According to Hunt, a young child's intelligence is not predetermined genetically at birth, but, rather, it is influenced to a great degree by the range of environmental encounters available to him. Bloom, in an analysis of test data on intelligence mentioned earlier, suggested that much of the variance in later tests of intelligence could be accounted for by variance in tests before the age of five. This study again supported those who argued for the use of early childhood education to compensate for cultural deficits in poor children.

These ideas represented one thrust in support of compensatory education. The view that education for young children should be supportive of development in nature was being challenged. There was a recognition of the impact of early experience that gave added impetus to the development of early childhood education. While growth could still be identified as the outcome of early education, as suggested by Johnson, the limits of growth were no longer considered to be predetermined. An interactionist approach to early education, whereby education was seen as stimulating rather than supporting development, began to replace the maturationist view as the central thrust of early childhood education. In addition, intellectual growth as well as social, emotional, and physical growth were seen as central to the program of early education. It is important to note that, while changes took place in psychologists' and educators' views of what areas of growth were important as well as what influenced or determined the ultimate development of the individual, the essential concern in terms of educational goals was to enhance development rather than to achieve specific learning outcomes.

Another thrust affecting early education programs grew out of the laboratory work of the behavioral psychologists. By manipulating the motivational sets of children and by dividing complex tasks into simpler components to be taught separately and later integrated, the behaviorists devised a technology that could be used to teach specific skills to young children. This work developed into a curriculum based upon a set of alternative propositions about the education of young children. Behavioral principles such as those proposed by Sidney Bijou and Donald Baer were used as the basis for systematic programs to teach specific skills and performances to children, including the young and the handicapped.[19]

A host of new curriculum conceptions and program models were developed during this period, many of which were generated in the research facilities of colleges and universities.[20] Often support for these developments relied on federal or foundation funds, and a number of the programs were integrated into the Planned Variations Program of Head Start and Follow-Through programs. The curriculum models have been implemented in varied geographic settings, and they have been supported over a period of time in order to assess the comparative effectiveness of each of the new approaches.

While each of the programs is unique, most have some essential elements in common with other program models so that they can be grouped together in a variety of ways. The range of these programs will ultimately narrow to allow concentration on just a few truly unique models.

All of the newer programs have been concerned essentially with ways of educating disadvantaged children. Some, like the Bereiter-Engelmann program, had as their source the identification of particular deficits that needed to be overcome.[21] While other programs have not been as specific in identifying deficits, all operate on the assumption that there are skills or attitudes and predispositions that can be learned at an early level, that can make a difference in the lives of children and in their later education, and that are important to children of poor and minority families. Parent participation is a common part of all programs in Head Start and Follow-Through.

It is beyond the scope of this chapter to present the content of various curriculum models presently available for early childhood education. Rather, the concern is with approaches used to analyze and compare divergent curriculum conceptions.

ANALYZING CURRICULUM CONCEPTIONS

Different schemes have been designed to identify similarities and differences among the various curriculum conceptions. These schemes require that early childhood programs be analyzed at various levels of abstraction. Kohlberg and Mayer, as noted earlier, suggest that programs differ on the basis of ideologies. Identifying three different ideological positions, they categorize the range of educational programs available. The report on early childhood education prepared by the Educational Products Information Exchange (EPIE) identifies three views of human development: behavioral-environmental, maturational-nativistic, and comprehensive-interactional. Using the EPIE framework, an individual, once he determines which view he prefers, can identify programs based upon similar views and select a proper program, at least from the point of view of consistency with psychological theory.[22] The views of human development presented in the EPIE document are similar to the ideological stands of the Kohlberg and Mayer article, which might suggest that psychological theories actually represent ideological positions. Practical and local considerations are also taken into account in the EPIE scheme.

The idea of philosophic or ideological issues intruding into or providing the basis for empirical or scientific thought is not a new one. Hans Furth suggests that the study of intelligence, basic to programs concerned with developing intelligence, is founded upon a philosophic question of what constitutes the nature of intelligence.[23] Thomas Kuhn goes even further and suggests that empirical science in general is based upon conceptual paradigms that are ideological in nature and do not grow out of the phenomena themselves.[24]

Another way of analyzing the ideological basis of school curricula has been suggested by James Macdonald. Building upon the work of Jürgen Habermus, Macdonald regards school programs as being built upon forms of knowledge that are based on human interests. Given this point of view, traditional early childhood programs can be identified as manifesting consensus interests. Innovative early childhood programs using behavioral principles can be identified as manifesting control interests. Early childhood programs oriented toward openness or self-reflection can be identified as manifesting liberation interests.[25]

In addition to curriculum analysis based upon ideological or philosophic bases, comparison of programs can be based on other attributes. David Weikart has categorized early childhood program models on the basis of conceptions of the role of the teacher and the role of the child as initiator or respondent. When a teacher initiates, she plans, organizes, and develops activities and lessons. When the teacher's role is to respond, she watches the children and responds to their needs. When a child initiates, he engages in direct experiences. When he responds, he is receptive to the teacher, carrying out her requests or demands. In a custodial program, according to Weikart, both teacher and child respond. In a child-centered program the child initiates, and the teacher responds. In a programmed curriculum, the teacher initiates, and the child responds. In an "open framework" curriculum both child and teacher initiate.[26] The framework Weikart uses resembles a conception used by Ann Bussis and Edward Chittendon to analyze open education. They identify programs as being either high or low in terms of the contributions of the student and the contributions of the teacher.[27] Some of the programs considered by Weikart to have "open frameworks," such as Susan Gray's DARCEE (Development and Research Center for Early Education) program or Merle Karne's Ameliorative curriculum, would be considered programmed by Bussis and Chittendon. The idea of categorizing programs according to the role of the teacher and the roles of the children can be a useful one, however.

Eleanor Maccoby and Miriam Zellner identify differences in Follow-Through programs based upon how learning is defined, how learning is viewed as occurring, and what is expected to be learned in each program. The use of incentives and conceptions of motivation are also seen as distinguishing features, along with various aspects of the classroom environment. In the area of learning theories, the Follow-Through programs seem to fall into two camps: one essentially following a Piagetian view of helping children acquire essential structures and operations; the other being concerned with producing observable changes in behavior. This essentially constitutes the distinction between growth-oriented and learning-oriented programs identified at the beginning of this chapter. It is this dimension that allows one to distinguish between the basic curriculum conceptions in the field of early childhood education. While all programs are concerned with intellectual and language skills, the skills that are considered important differ from program to program, as do strategies for teaching those skills. The strategies can range from patterned drills to the creation of environments to induce language and cognitive behavior, often through play. As for motivation, one set of programs is based upon external reinforcement, which means that children are rewarded for appropriate behavior with tokens or snacks or opportunities to play. The other set of programs relies on intrinsic motivation or the attempt to make learning activities rewarding in themselves.[28]

Other schemes have been devised to help identify important distinctions among early childhood education programs. Ronald Parker and Mary Day analyzed a range of preschool programs in terms of major goals as well as objectives in the areas of sensory-motor skills, cognition, language, socioemotional development, and academic content. All programs do not include objectives in all of these areas, however. They also examined implementation procedures, including the age of the intended clients, the instructional format used (for example, direct, dialogic, teacher-directed, planned environment), the teacher's role in instruction, the grouping of children, the sequence of activities, and the use of parental participation. In addition, they attempted to assess the structural level for children and teachers in the program, the role of the teacher, and the conceptions of motivation used.[29]

The following framework for analysis of programs suggests that certain components in each program be identified in order to make satisfactory judgments about similarities and differences:

1. Assumptions
    1.1 Assumptions about the client
    1.2 Assumptions about the educative process
    1.3 Assumptions about the school
    1.4 Assumptions about the teacher
2. Goals of the program
    2.1 Long range goals
    2.2 Short term objectives
    2.3 Relationship between the two
    2.4 The degree of specificity of objectives
3. Curriculum
    3.1 Range of content of the program
    3.2 Sequence of learnings or experiences
4. Method
    4.1 Child-child transactions
    4.2 Child-teacher transactions
    4.3 Child-materials transactions
    4.4 Explicitness of prescriptions
5. Style
6. Organization
    6.1 Scheduling
    6.2 Spatial organization

This framework can be used to analyze and evaluate a program model that is intended to be copied or emulated by identifying essential elements and relationships in the program. A program model, however, is a representation of reality rather than reality itself. When models are implemented, idealized forms can be distorted or changed. Some models are also more difficult to implement than others. Program models cannot be evaluated as to outcome, but actual program implementations can. Such evaluations of program outcomes provide a measure of program effectiveness. Several programs have been tested as to effectiveness, and a number of programs have been evaluated in parallel situations so that outcomes can be compared.

EVALUATING CURRICULUM CONCEPTIONS

Karnes evaluated a Bereiter-Engelmann program, an Ameliorative program, a traditional program, a Montessori program, and a community-based program and assessed outcomes based upon tests of intelligence and of achievement. In the early data collections, the Bereiter-Engelmann and Ameliorative programs, both highly structured and consistent with behavioral principles, produced the greatest gains on standardized tests scores, although these differences lessened over time.[31] Weikart compared a Bereiter-Engelmann program, a Piaget-based program, and a traditional program designed for disadvantaged children. The assessment of outcomes in this study was based on intelligence tests as well as observations and ratings. The findings showed that children in each program did well, but no one program was superior to any other as to outcome. Weikart suggests that it is the staff planning and continued supervision of teachers rather than program models that make an educational difference.[32]

One of the more extensive attempts to evaluate curriculum conceptions in early childhood education can be found in the Planned Variations Program of Project Follow-Through. Different curriculum models have been implemented in varied settings over a long period of time. All of the children are from disadvantaged backgrounds, and different cultures are represented in different communities. Outcome data are being collected on both academic and nonacademic variables.

In a study of the two-year effects of the various models on academic achievement, it was found that three of the models, representing a behavioral program, an open education program, and a bilingual program, showed positive effects when compared with non-Follow-Through control children. Three others, including a behavioral program, a responsive program, and a developmental program, showed lesser effects. Four programs that showed little change after two years also included a behavioral program, an open education program, a developmental program, and a Piagetian program. Because programs were implemented as totalities, it was not possible to determine if differences could be attributed to curriculum model dimensions, implementation dimensions, or other factors. There were major site effects, which suggests that site dynamics and population characteristics do much to mediate program effects.[33] Perhaps model implementation procedures and curriculum components should be viewed simply as sets of variables within educational interactions when evaluating curriculum constructions in actual operation.

Louise Miller and Jean Dyer studied four preschool programs and their effects as they related to disadvantaged children in Louisville. The programs studied were Bereiter-Engelmann, DARCEE, Montessori, and a "traditional" early childhood program. Unlike the studies discussed earlier, there was long-term follow-up evaluation. Miller and Dyer summarize their conclusion as follows:

With respect to program effects: (a) The prekindergarten programs did have different effects on children, both in terms of immediate impact and over a 4-year period regardless of what programs they had later. (b) For all prekindergarten programs, the immediate impact on cognitive variables was in predictable directions, with higher levels of IQ and achievement resulting from programs which emphasized these goals. (c) Those prekindergarten program effects which were still detectable after a 4-year period were in the "noncognitive" areas. (d) The most consistent and beneficial effects of these prekindergarten programs occurred for males. (e) Children from all programs declined in IQ over the 4-year period, but the children from the prekindergarten program which had the greatest immediate impact on IQ and achievement declined most. (f) There were virtually no main effects on noncognitive variables which could be attributed to the kindergarten, first-grade, or second-grade programs. (g) Differential effects on both cognitive and noncognitive variables did result from various combinations of prekindergarten and kindergarten programs.[34]

Miller and Dyer's study demonstrates that there are different outcomes from different treatments, although differences may not be large or hold up over time. Differences in noncognitive effects were also evident. This study again points to the need to look at compounding effects that education after the preschool period has on the outcomes of preschool programs, a consideration often not taken into account in evaluating outcomes of early childhood programs.

One of the difficulties in assessing the worth of programs is in evaluating the outcomes. Edna Shapiro addresses the problem of evaluation later in this volume.[35] Not only are there problems of validity and reliability concerned with using assessment instruments for young children, but there are no instruments to measure certain kinds of outcomes. Intelligence tests are difficult to administer to young children, especially when the subjects belong to a different cultural or class group from that of the person administering the test. An even more serious problem rests with whether there is acceptance of the basic assumption that intelligence tests are useful in providing an assessment of individual intelligence. The use of intelligence tests and other standardized tests to evaluate children at all levels of schooling is being questioned today.[36]

Possibly a more important problem rests in the basic distinction between the goals of different kinds of early childhood programs. Two separate approaches to early childhood education have emerged over time, and there are variations within each approach. Many programs consider their basic goal to be the support and stimulation of development in children. These programs do not specify any particular behavior as a goal. As in Johnson's nursery school, they may be concerned with predispositions or attitudes, or, as in Piagetian programs, with the creation of internal structures and operations. Any number of behavioral manifestations might be representative of an internal structure, and a particular behavior might be elicited without the concomitant internal structure developing. Behaviors, therefore, may not identify the achievement of "real goals" of the program, even though they do indicate goal achievement. Early childhood curriculum conceptions that set growth as their goal date back as far as Froebel, and they continue through the Macmillan Nursery School to modern curriculum constructions.

The other approach to the education of young children rejects the use of the development of internal structures or predispositions as appropriate goals of education. Instead, the goals are stated as behaviors or skills that are observable and can be taught by direct or indirect training. These programs go back as far as Montessori and can be found still in the conduct curriculum of Patty Hill, as well as in modern behavior-oriented programs.

It is relatively simple to evaluate achievement in performance-oriented programs. Because the behavior is observable, one can judge whether goals are achieved or not through direct observation. The level of inference needed is low. It is a much more difficult matter to assess growth. Growth is gradual, and many external as well as internal conditions contribute over time. Growth is also often internal and not directly observable so that only indirect indicators are possible. A high level of inference is required in this kind of assessment, with observable data used as the basis for such inference. It is difficult to identify the long-term consequences of any set of programs or the antecedents of any growth spurt. It is even more difficult to partial out the effects of intervening experiences. This does not mean that the latter forms of programs should be discarded because evaluation is difficult or that former kinds of programs are more worthy. Even in a behaviorally oriented program, the value of any particular set of behaviors established as the goals of the program is usually instrumental: the outcomes are considered worthy because they support and encourage the more mature kinds of behavior that are the ultimate goal of education. Relationships between short-term objectives and long-range goals are often more logical than empirical in their support.

In a sense, then, all program construction in early childhood education represents an act of faith in regard to long-range effects, a faith that cannot easily be tested in the confusing, confounding real world. This does not suggest that educators should stop long- or short-term evaluation; instead, they should recognize the limitations of those activities.

In addition to being a statement of faith, early childhood programs are also statements of values. Curriculum constructions at the early childhood level, as at all other levels, are designed to influence chil-

dren, to somehow make them something other than they might otherwise have been. Some programs are designed to make children more
competent elementary students, not only in terms of academic skills
but also in terms of becoming familiar with the elementary system.
Other programs are designed to make children more creative or to be
more effective citizens. At an earlier time I suggested that an appropriate goal of early childhood education would be to help children
develop a greater degree of personal autonomy but autonomy based
upon reason,[37] an idea proposed by R. F. Dearden. This autonomy
would require two elements: (1) an independence of authorities, and
(2) the personal testing of the truth of things, then forming intentions
and choosing according to a personal scale of values. Reason is needed
to make choices and identify values if selection is to be independent of
authority.[38] Gerald Ashby suggests that such a goal represents an ethical principle arising from basic values in Western civilization.[39] Personal freedom, or autonomy, is an ethical good and therefore an
independent principle to be valued in its own right. Autonomy or
freedom, as described above, has both a negative and a positive facet.
The negative side, independence from authority, suggests freedom
from external imposition. The positive side, the testing of truth and
choosing and acting based upon this testing, suggests a freedom to do
things for oneself. Often those responsible for developing a curriculum
have concerned themselves with only one of the facets. Those concerned with supporting growth have promoted the absence of external
control, allowing the child freedom to be, while those concerned with
the learning of particular skills have stressed the need for learning
competencies, allowing the child freedom to do. Each of these limited
views of freedom, when considered alone, is inadequate to support a
view of autonomy as suggested above.

If we accept the assumption that early childhood programs are
manifestations of ethical principles, then analysis and evaluation of
such programs must be based as much on the ethical worth of program activities and their outcomes as on their effectiveness, no matter
what evaluative measure is used. But the evaluation used must take
into consideration the total ethical position, as well as the total context
of each curriculum constructed in early childhood education.

Notes

1. Marvin Lazerson, "The Historical Antecedents of Early Childhood Education," in *Early Childhood Education*, ed. Ira J. Gordon, Seventy-first Yearbook of the National Society of the Study of Education, Part II, (Chicago: University of Chicago Press, 1972), 33–35.

2. Benjamin S. Bloom, *Stability and Change in Human Characteristics* (New York: John Wiley & Sons, 1964).

3. Benjamin C. Gregory, "The Necessity of Continuity between the Kindergarten and the Elementary Schools: The Present Status Illogical and Un-Froebelian," in *The Co-ordination of the Kindergarten and the Elementary School*, Seventh Yearbook of the National Society for the Study of Education, Part II (Chicago: University of Chicago Press, 1908), 22–34.

4. *Friedrich Froebel, A Selection from His Writings*, ed. Irene Lilly (Cambridge, Eng.: Cambridge University Press, 1967).

5. See *Froebel and English Education*, ed. Evelyn Lawrence (New York: Schocken Books, 1969); and Evelyn Weber, *The Kindergarten: Its Encounter with Educational Thought in America* (New York: Teachers College Press, Columbia University, 1969).

6. Maria Montessori, *The Montessori Method* (New York: Schocken Books, 1969), 119–345.

7. Margaret Macmillan, *The Nursery School* (London: J. M. Dent & Sons, 1919), 83–153.

8. Weber, *The Kindergarten*, 126–175.

9. D. Bruce Gardner, *Development in Early Childhood: The Preschool Years* (New York: Harper & Row, 1964), 5–17.

10. Lawrence Kohlberg and Rochelle Mayer, "Development as the Aim of Education," *Harvard Educational Review* 42 (November 1972): 449–496.

11. Harriet Johnson, *School Begins at Two* (New York: Agathon Press, 1970; originally published in 1936), 6.

12. *Ibid.*, 7.

13. *Ibid.*, 67.

14. Roma Gans, Celia Burns Stendler, and Millie Almy, *Teaching Young Children in Nursery School, Kindergarten and the Primary Grades* (Yonkers-on-Hudson, N.Y.: World Book Co., 1952), 80–81.

15. *Ibid.*, 82–85.

16. Fred L. Strodtbeck, "The Hidden Curriculum of the Middle Class Home," in *Education of the Disadvantaged*, eds. A. Harry Passow, Miriam Goldberg, and Abraham J. Tannenbaum (New York: Holt, Rinehart and Winston, 1967), 244–260.

17. Basil Bernstein, "Social Class and Linguistic Development: A Theory of Social Learning," in *Education, Economy and Society*, eds. A. H. Halsey, Jean Floud, and C. Arnold Anderson (Glencoe, Ill.: Free Press, 1961), 288–314.

18. J. McVicker Hunt, *Intelligence and Experience* (New York: Ronald Press, 1961).

19. Sidney W. Bijou and Donald M. Baer, *Child Development I: A Systematic and Empirical Theory* (New York: Appleton-Century-Crofts, 1961).

20. For a review and analysis of these programs, see Ellis D. Evans, *Contemporary Influences in Early Childhood Education*, 2d ed. (New York: Holt, Rinehart and Winston, 1975); Ronald K. Parker, ed., *The Preschool in Action* (Boston: Allyn & Bacon, 1972); Bernard Spodek, *Early Childhood Education* (Englewood Cliffs, N.J.: Prentice-Hall, 1973).

21. Carl Bereiter and Siegfried Engelmann, *Teaching Disadvantaged Children in the Preschool* (Englewood Cliffs, N.J.: Prentice-Hall, 1966).

22. *Early Childhood Education: How to Select and Evaluate Materials*, Educational Product Report Number 24 (New York: Educational Products Information Exchange Institute, 1972).

23. Hans G. Furth, *Piaget and Knowledge: Theoretical Foundations* (Englewood Cliffs, N.J.: Prentice-Hall, 1969), 4.

24. Thomas S. Kuhn, *The Structure of Scientific Revolutions*, 2d ed. (Chicago: University of Chicago Press, 1970).

25. Bernard Spodek, "Early Childhood Education and Teacher Education: A Search for Consistency," *Young Children* 30 (March 1975): 168-173.

26. David P. Weikart, "Relationship of Curriculum, Teaching and Learning in Preschool Education," in *Preschool Programs for the Disadvantaged*, ed. Julian C. Stanley (Baltimore, Md.: Johns Hopkins University Press, 1972), 29-37.

27. Ann M. Bussis and Edward A. Chittendon, *Analysis of an Approach to Open Education* (Princeton, N.J.: Educational Testing Service, 1970).

28. Eleanor E. Maccoby and Miriam Zellner, *Experiments in Primary Education: Aspects of Project Follow-Through* (New York: Harcourt Brace Jovanovich, 1970).

29. Ronald K. Parker and Mary C. Day, "Comparison of Preschool Curricula," in *The Preschool in Action: Exploring Early Childhood Programs*, ed. Ronald K. Parker (Boston: Allyn & Bacon, 1972), 466-506.

30. Spodek, *Early Childhood Education*, 30-31.

31. Merle Karnes, Audrey S. Hodgins, James A. Teska, and Samuel A. Kirk, *Research and Development Program on Preschool Disadvantaged Children*, Vol. I (Washington, D.C.: U. S. Office of Education, 1969).

32. Weikart, "Relationship of Curriculum Teaching and Learning," 38-57.

33. Marvin G. Cline et al., *Education as Experimentation: Evaluation of the Follow-Through Planned Variation Model*. Vol. IIA, *Two Year Effects of the Follow-Through* (Cambridge, Mass.: Abt Associates, 1975).

34. Louise B. Miller and Jean L. Dyer, *Four Preschool Programs: Their Dimensions and Effects*, Monograph No. 162, *Monographs of the Society for Research in Child Development* 40 (October 1975), 136-137.

35. See Chapter 10.

36. See *I.Q.: The Myth of Measurability*, *National Elementary Principal* 54 (March- April 1975): entire issue; and *The Scoring of Children: Standardized Testing in America, ibid.*, 54 (July-August 1975): entire issue.

37. Bernard Spodek, "What Are the Sources of Early Childhood Curriculum?" *Young Children* 26 (October 1970): 48-58.

38. R. F. Dearden, *The Philosophy of Primary Education* (London: Routledge and Kegan Paul, 1968), 46.

39. Gerald Ashby, *Preschool Theories and Strategies* (Melbourne, Australia: Melbourne University Press, 1972).

9. Behavior Analysis Applied to Early Childhood Education

Sidney W. Bijou

Fifty years from now it is both possible and likely that educators will claim that preschool is the most important single educational experience in the life of a child. It is currently accepted, almost without exception, that the preschool years constitute one of the most important stages of human development. It would follow that, when a truly effective approach to teaching in the preschool years is achieved, the preschool period should be the most significant and influential in a child's life. If one accepts this line of reasoning, the problems of preschool education should be considered in light of the most reliable knowledge of human behavior and development—in other words, in light of the concepts, principles, and methodology of behavior analysis.

The application of behavioral principles to preschool education is by no means a recent innovation. It is, in fact, as old as the original behavioristic brand of functionalism. At the turn of the century Patty Smith Hill, a follower of John Dewey, John B. Watson, and Edward L. Thorndike, contended that the kindergarten curriculum should develop from the subject matter of the school, the developmental status of the children, and the history and future potentialities of society.[1] She maintained, further, that the method of teaching should be based on "habit" training, very much in the mode of Watson.[2] The present-day behavioral approach to preschool education is clearly manifested in the work of many, including Donald Bushell; Barbara Etzel, Nancy Bybel, Karen Busby, Lois Dixon, and Joseph Spradlin; Todd Risley, Nancy Reynolds, and Betty Hart; and Carolyn Thomson.[3] The theoretical underpinning of the work of these investigators relies heavily not on Watson but on B. F. Skinner, who integrated Thorndike's theory of trial-and-error learning and Pavlov's concept of classical conditioning into a system for the understanding of human behavior.[4]

The behavioral influence can be seen in other approaches to preschool education, among them, the Bereiter-Engelmann structured program, the early training project known as DARCEE (Demonstration and Research Center for Early Childhood), and the Tucson early educational model.[5] This chapter focuses on the behavioral approach to preschool education as it affects the philosophy or the goals of teaching, the methods used in teaching or the means of achieving preschool goals, and the support needed by teachers to perform their jobs to the extent of their training.

PHILOSOPHY OF PRESCHOOL EDUCATION: THE GOALS OF TEACHING

Everyone—parent, older sibling, relative, friend, or teacher—who helps a young child learn has some kind of philosophy of education. For parents and older siblings (really parent aides), the goals are implicit or "natural" to the practices of the family and consist of helping the child to learn self-care skills and to achieve the beginnings of social, cognitive, and moral behavior. For relatives and friends, the goals are also implicit and "natural" to practices of the extended family and the neighborhood, practices that lead to the achievement of certain broader social and recreational abilities and knowledge. The goals of preschool teachers are, on the other hand, explicit. They have some kind of child development rationale, and they are linked to educational materials and methods and form a curriculum that focuses primarily on the child's verbal abilities and knowledge and on his social-emotional needs.

Preschool Goals Are Value Judgments

Regardless of the teacher, the setting, and the degree of explicitness, the goals of teaching are value judgments about what the behavior of a child should be; they are by no means conclusions drawn

directly from research, whether it be educational, sociological, psy-
chiatric, or psychological.[6] The goals for preschool education are
based on ideological or philosophical conceptions of the child, the
society, and the role of preschool education in that society. Those who
should be responsible for selecting goals are parents, teachers, school
administrators, members of boards of education, and governmental
officials. Experts in early childhood education serve, or should serve,
primarily as resource persons who provide the decision makers with
information on human development, learning, adjustment, and instructional process, the workings and future directions of society, the
benefits and risks of particular educational practices, methods of
evaluating educational programs, and the principles of the decision-
making process itself.

Advice from professional educators about preschool goals has been
divergent, conflicting, and confusing. There are those who hold that
the goals should depend entirely on the psychological needs of the
child. At the same time others maintain that the needs of society
should be the sole determining factor. Educators who espouse child-
centered goals generally hold that a child is born with built-in, self-
actualizing tendencies and that one should leave the child to his own
devices in discovering his naturally constructive nature. Such educators support unstructured teaching programs, and present-day advocates of something akin to Froebelian doctrine include the Piagetians,
with their hypothetical cognitive structures and processes evolving
through predetermined stages;[7] the neo-Freudians, with their concepts
of the development of the components of personality structure (id,
ego, and superego and the evolution of the sense of trust, autonomy,
and initiative);[8] and the Gesellians, with their notions about the
growth of the mind, manifested to motor, social, adaptive, and language development.[9] Cognitive structures, the components of personality structure, and parallel divisions of the mind are hypothetical internal causal entities, inferred from behavior and preconceptions
about the original nature of man. They exist only in the behavior of
the theorists, that is to say, in their writings and lectures. When the
theories that they espouse lose their credibility, nursery school goals
based upon such theories also become meaningless because the hypothetical terms and relationships upon which they depend become nonfunctional when it is demonstrated that preschool goals and the means
of achieving them can be stated in terms of observable behavior.

Educators who hold that preschool goals must be based not on the needs of the child but on the needs of society contend that a child is naturally unsocial or antisocial and that if he is not given a structured school situation, such as occurs with the Bereiter-Engelmann program,[10] he fails to acquire behaviors essential for societal living. This rationalization carries over from the days when parents used children, as soon as they were physically able, to augment the economic resources of the family. In the preindustrial period, prior to the delegation of education to a social agency, children automatically joined their parents in helping the family to survive, a practice that constituted a most important part of the offsprings' education and training. With the onset of the industrial age and the establishment of community schools, the pressing of children into large-scale farm operations and factories proved hazardous to children. Ultimately there were laws forbidding such practices. This broader social view of the goals of education coincides with the belief held by certain religious groups that a child is sinful by nature.

It is my contention that any acceptable philosophy of preschool education must take into account both the developmental status of the child and the characteristics of his society. This position is not derived from a pragmatic attempt to make the best of both worlds. It relies, instead, on the natural science assumption that a child develops, or changes progressively, as a consequence of interactions with the environment and therefore that *the development of a child cannot ever be considered separately from the specific events that constitute his environment.* The behavior displayed by a child entering nursery school is the result of interaction between his own unique biological makeup (including natural bodily changes or biological maturation) and specific events encountered since the day he was born. By the time he finishes nursery school, his behavior is a function of his unique biological makeup and interactions among specific events not only in his home but also in the nursery school and the immediate community. These streams of interactions make the child the "personality" that he is at any stage in his development.

The goals of the preschool, like the goals of any school, should help the child develop behaviors that relate to his current environment and to situations he can expect in his life. Behaviors should, moreover, aim at enhancing the development of both child and society, at helping each to grow stronger and to survive. Although "enhancing the strength and the survival possibilities of a society" has a somewhat lofty sound, it actually ranges from simply managing one's own affairs to spearheading innovations that could benefit society as a whole. Helping a child derive satisfaction from living and developing and at the same time preparing him to participate and to contribute to the welfare of society are compatible goals.

Goals based on a child's current interactions with the environment should be compatible with practices in both the home and the community. As for goals based on home practices, the question that confronts us is: How effective are current parent programs, first, in conveying to the nursery school staff the practices of the home and, second, in helping the staff integrate the practices of home and school? Goals based on practices in the immediate community are achieved mainly through direct contact with institutions of community living such as shopping centers, power plants, and bus terminals, in conjunction with discussions about how they function.

Preschool goals based on future situations should include behaviors that will help a child cope with the practices of the kindergarten or first grade he is likely to attend and with the social activities that probably foreshadow changes in his culture. Several semibehavioral preschool programs focus on just such goals. "In most of the programs of early childhood education, goals are stated in terms of the behaviors necessary for success in later schooling. These might be cognitive skills as in the DARCEE program, or academic skills as in the Bereiter-Engelmann-Becker-program, or a combination of social skills necessary for the role of student and academic skills as in the Behavior Analysis program."[11] It is obvious that goals of this sort are desirable, but they should constitute only a part of the objectives of preschool education.

Preschool goals relating to preparing a child for probable future changes in society are more difficult to attain than those geared to his current situation because knowledge about teaching problem-solving behavior is limited and the nature of future events is uncertain. Preschool programs should, nevertheless, include goals pertaining to the teaching of problem-solving techniques, at least to the extent of our present knowledge. They should also include activities that have implications for life in the future, such as space exploration, developments in electronics, and concern about food supply and distribution, energy shortages, ecology, and international relationships.

Behaviorally Oriented Preschool Goals

Those responsible for selecting goals for a preschool program traditionally make collective decisions based on the objectives of preschools already in operation (especially demonstration schools), on the literature available on early childhood education, on family and community considerations, on economic factors, and on consultation with educators and other professionals. If a behavior analyst were to advise such a group, he would recommend a set of goals that would emphasize the furthering of individuality and of problem-solving ability through the development of abilities and knowledge, the extension of motivations, and the enhancement of self-management skills. The specific items under each of the following headings are not viewed as immutable but as alterable in light of further research. The items do indicate change in society, where it is (its image), and where it is probably heading.

Development of Abilities and Knowledge

Ability and knowledge goals imply that the child will be taught how to do things and how to acquire information about objects, people, occurrences, and himself, that is, his self-concept.[12] These goals fall into ten subclasses. The first four pertain to behavior primarily in relation to self; the last six, to behavior mainly in relation to society. The subclasses are listed as:
1. body management and control, including manual dexterity and locomotor skills;
2. physical health and safety;
3. self-care, including dressing, undressing, and toilet training;
4. recreation and play;
5. social behavior, including all forms of communication;
6. aesthetic knowledge and abilities in relation to art, crafts, music, and literature;
7. everyday mechanical skills;
8. knowledge of community services (for example, transportation, sanitation, fire fighting);
9. preacademic and academic subjects; and
10. methods and content of science.

Extension of Motivations

In technical behavioral terms the extension of motives, in the form of attitudes, interests, and values, involves replacing appetitive and aversive contingencies with positive, conditioned reinforcers: specific generalized, extrinsic, and intrinsic. In psychoanalytic terms, the objective is to change behavior motivated by id forces to behavior motivated by ego and superego impulses. Goals in the behavioral sense include:

1. preservation and extension of moral values in keeping with the family moral code and the moral code of the classroom as a subculture;
2. preservation and extension of ecological (natural) reinforcers, and, by definition, preservation and extension of exploratory behavior;
3. development of positive attitudes toward and interests in people as individuals and as groups; and
4. positive attitudes toward and interests in attending school and in the activities of school and community.

Enhancement of Self-Management Skills

This third category of objectives refers to the acquisition of self-management skills in the broadest sense. These skills are usually deemed desirable because they are said to enhance innovative behavior, self-control, and problem-solving ability. They consist of the beginning stages of:

1. personal self-management techniques including the development of desirable "personal habits," "moral habits," and "work habits," as well as the ability to concentrate on the subject at hand and work independently and systematically (development of autonomy); and
2. problem solving (thinking) and decision-making skills, including creative and innovative behavior.

TEACHING METHODS: MEANS OF ACHIEVING GOALS

From the dawn of human culture there have been highly effective teachers who achieve their effectiveness "on their own" or through the specific contingencies that constitute their personal histories. With the advent of an applied science of human behavior, competent teachers can be trained to be even more effective, and less competent teachers can be trained to perform their job adequately.

The notion that a teacher can be trained leads one to question learning models offered in teacher training. One example is the *experience* model, which emphasizes exposing a child to a great variety of

stimulating experiences. Then there is the *doing* model, which encourages all sorts of activity, especially exploratory behavior. Another
example is the *trial-and-error* model, which affords a child opportunities to interact with objects and people in order to learn from "feedback," that is, the consequences of his actions. One final example is
the *open situation* model, which provides a child with physical and
social environments that encourage desirable behavior to evolve
naturally.

Each of these models is inadequate because each stresses only a
single aspect of learning. In the experience model it is the material to
be learned or the task to be performed that is emphasized. In the doing model the behavioral component receives most of the attention. In
the trial-and-error model it is the consequences of the behavior that
are paramount. In the open situation model the setting for learning is
stressed.

There is another model, based on modern behavior theory, that
brings together all four components, and teaching is defined as the arrangement of the components in a way that facilitates learning.[13] The
selection and sequencing of the material or procedure, and the techniques used for presentation (for example, priming, modeling, fading, and rule giving), require actual experience. The behavioral aspect enters into the shaping of behavior or the development of motor
and verbal abilities and skills. The consequences of behavior relate to
the management of reinforcing contingencies, including their proper
selection and use in developing personal traits (for example, autonomy) and new reinforcers (new interests). And, finally, it is the setting
or contextual component that allows control of the entire situation to
promote educationally desirable behavior throughout a school day.

A child is, of course, perfectly capable of learning without a teacher
and should be given ample opportunity and encouraged to do so. But
the learning of many abilities and much knowledge does require a
teacher because the reinforcement contingencies involved do not ordi-
narily occur naturally (as in concept formation), or because the contingencies are too remote to influence appropriate behavior (as in
learning to avoid poisonous plants).

Applied Behavior Analysis Teaching Strategy

Applied behavior analysis teaching strategy, which is always directed to an individual child, has been described in the educational liter-

ature in many different ways. The strategy, it seems, consists of five basic phases: specifying or clarifying the goals of teaching in observable terms; beginning instruction at the child's level of competence; arranging the teaching situation (materials, procedures, instructions, setting, and contingencies) to facilitate learning in directions that enhance the individuality of a child; monitoring progress and altering materials and procedures to advance learning; and following practices that generalize, elaborate, and maintain the behaviors acquired.

It has already been stated that the goals of preschool teaching are, or should be, established by a representative group of people, with parents having a clear and strong voice. The goals should stem from their understanding of the child, of the society, and of the role of preschool education in that society. The teacher's main function then becomes the division of each general goal into logical subdivisions and subgoals that are appropriate for each child and that heighten each child's individuality.

To begin a teaching program at a child's level of competence, the teacher must first assess the child's preinstructional behavior (competencies) in relevant areas, that is, the teacher makes an educational diagnosis. Criterion-referenced tests, which provide information on social and cognitive repertoires, are more useful in making the diagnosis than norm-referenced tests, which yield data on mental age, social age, intelligence, or grade achievement.[14]

The teacher plans and selects those materials, activities, and situations that, under most conditions, will lead to reaching the preestablished goal. When planning art experiences, for example, three kinds of art activities must be considered: those that allow freedom to combine elements, those that deal with the development of skills and discriminations, and those that are craft-oriented. The teacher should use techniques that encourage original productions stemming from the child's personal history and encourage him to interact with the materials, her instructions, and the reinforcers.[15]

Keeping samples of productions, such as handwriting and artwork, and of records that show each child's social behaviors, such as initiating conversation with a peer, provides the teacher with a systematic account of progress. Based on this data, the teacher can reevaluate the programming of material, the physical setting, the instructions, and the effectiveness of the reinforcers.

Lastly, the teacher incorporates into daily teaching plans those activities that generalize, elaborate, and maintain the abilities and knowledge that the child has acquired. This can be done in the school setting by posing problems and questions in contexts that differ from the learning situation and by reinforcing instances of related learned behaviors that occur "spontaneously," but are not arranged by the teacher. The teacher can also work with the mother and demonstrate how to help a child generalize, elaborate, and maintain school-learned behavior at home.

Behavior acquired in a learning situation generalizes to other situations, or, stated more precisely, learned behavior automatically comes under the control of stimuli similar to those in the learning situation. But effective teaching, whether by teachers or parents, increases the probability of generalization, mainly through practices that strengthen learned behaviors. For example, contingencies can be arranged that teach cooperative behavior in the preschool during group activities, recess, snack time, and art class. There are similar opportunities at home while playing, cleaning up, eating, and performing chores. The elaborating of learned behavior actually refers to the arranging of contingencies so as to transform learned behavior into more complex forms: extending walking to hopping, skipping, and jumping; expanding one-word sentences to phrases and longer sentences.

Maintaining learned behavior, often referred to as improving memory or retention, consists of arranging reinforcing contingencies so that learned behavior preserves its strength. Once a child is taught to remove his coat and hang it up, he should be encouraged by a pleasant remark, or a pat on the back so that he will continue this practice whenever he enters the house. The key principle underlying this aspect of applied behavioral analysis teaching strategy is to distribute reinforcement on a schedule that will keep the behavior vigorous, starting with frequent reinforcement and gradually reducing the frequency.

Applying Behavioral Teaching Strategy to Preschool Situations

The effectiveness of the application of the behavior strategy to teaching specific objectives ultimately depends upon the teacher's dedication to achieving curriculum goals and her skill in applying behavior principles to develop the individuality of each child in her class. It is agreed almost unanimously that the teacher is the most important factor in any teaching situation since she is the one who has direct contact with the child. Research has shown, however, that the correlation between teacher characteristics and pupil accomplishment and achievement is close to zero. This astonishing fact calls for new ways of conceptualizing the teacher and the teaching process.[16] A measure of effectiveness that should be explored is how well a teacher applies principles of behavior and development. If she is skillful, continually rearranging the teaching situation to suit the child's progress as recorded in objective terms, there should be a substantial positive relationship between her teaching behavior and pupil achievement and school attitudes.

Development of Abilities and Knowlege

Teaching both the abilities and the knowledge required to deal with the ten behavior subgroups mentioned earlier involves the effective management of reinforcing contingencies. The key procedure for teaching ability categories is differential reinforcement of successive approximations to the form of the goal response. Working with a young child faced with the task of learning how to draw a circle, the teacher reinforces him first as he learns more efficient ways of holding the pencil, and then of drawing curved lines that more closely approximate those of a circle, until he eventually draws an acceptable circle. This procedure is referred to as response differentiation or shaping.[17] To say that the key principle in teaching abilities and skills involves reinforcing successive changes in response form does not imply that the occasion (discriminative stimulus or cue) and context (setting factor) can be ignored. An ability is always taught in relation to some situation (the ability to draw is taught in relation to a pencil or crayon and a sheet of paper) and a favorable context (a quiet and relaxed setting) for performing that task.

The fundamental procedure for teaching knowledge categories is discrimination training or differential reinforcement on the basis of an occasion (discriminative stimulus or cue). Sometimes the occasion for differential reinforcement is the action of a person, such as extending the hand to greet someone; sometimes it is one or several aspects of two stimulus complexes, such as teaching a child to discriminate between an apple and an orange; sometimes it is abstraction, such as teaching "in-front-of" spatial relations and other concepts.[18] The form of knowledge behavior, which ranges from a simple pointing response to a complex verbal structure (interactional chain), and the setting factors for learning are also factors to be considered in the teaching of knowledge.

There is an additional significant and essential point about the teaching of abilities and knowledge. *The achievement of the other two categories of goals—motivations and self-management skills—depends to a large extent on techniques used to teach the abilities and knowledge categories.* In other words, abilities and knowledge taught according to the principles described here serve to extend and elaborate motives and to strengthen self-control and self-management skills.

Extension of Motivations

Procedures that the teacher uses in teaching abilities and knowledge can make the activity, the situation, and even the teacher distasteful to a child. Even though a student responds as required and the teacher works diligently at presenting, explaining, repeating, and reviewing, teaching procedures might rouse little enthusiasm for learning. It is possible, however, for teaching procedures to rouse enthusiasm for the activity, the situation, and the teacher, and, ultimately, for learning.

Teaching designed to extend moral values and positive attitudes toward peers and adults, school and school activities, and ecological (natural) reinforcers involves the skillful management of positive reinforcers in ways that establish new positive conditioned reinforcers for a child.[19] The extension of moral values depends largely on clearly specifying the behaviors classified as "good" and applying positive contingencies when they occur and on specifying "bad" behaviors and applying either no contingencies at all or techniques of self-control, including mild reprimands, when they take place.[20]

The teaching of positive attitudes toward peers and adults, both as individuals and as members of groups, involves pairing the activities of peers and adults with social or physical stimuli (including activities) that are meaningful (functional) for a child. Since most children enter nursery school with positive attitudes toward their peers, the teacher, and aides, training for a child with negative attitudes is usually categorized as remedial.

To teach positive attitudes toward attending school, reinforcers must be paired with coming to school. The first step in planning the program is an assessment of the child's attendance record. "Liking for school" might be evaluated by the rate and regularity of school attendance, crying (frequency and duration) or smiling upon arrival at school, the parents' report of the child's eagerness (or reluctance) to go to school, or whether the opportunity to attend school could be used to reinforce other low frequency behavior in the home, such as eating breakfast, putting away pajamas, or helping to make the bed. The desired goal for a child who cries each time he comes to school would, of course, be to have him arrive at school in a "good," that is, cheerful and eager, frame of mind.

The principle involved in developing a child's interests in nonpreferred school activities is the establishing of intrinsic reinforcers that come from participation in the activity. The conditioned reinforcing properties of school actitivtes can be assessed when a child first enters school by measuring the time spent at a given task without prompts, primes, or reinforcement from the teacher, or by recording choice or preference when the child is given an opportunity to select an activity. Then there is a need to provide social or other contrived reinforcers to responses to school tasks. Finally there is a need to fade these response contingencies on a percentage reinforcement schedule, that is, on a schedule that starts with 100 percent pairing and is gradually reduced to some value such as 30 percent, so that the activity itself, and in some cases its products, develops conditioned reinforcement properties. For example, performing an activity such as painting "art" products that are viewed with approval by the teacher, the teacher's aide, and parents will, after such training, become automatically reinforcing providing approval is functionally reinforcing for the child. To maintain this behavior, occasional social reinforcers are also required.

The strengthening of ecological (natural) reinforcers requires opportunities for the child to engage in exploratory behavior in physical environments highly responsive to his overtures at times when he is alert, rested, has no need for food, drink, toileting, and the like, that is, when he is free from appetitive and aversive stimulations.[21] It also involves using ecological reinforcers, whenever possible, in the teaching of any school subject. In teaching rhythms, for example, it is simple to arrange conditions so that the sounds the child produces are exciting and naturally reinforcing.

Enhancement of Self-Management Skills

The enhancement of self-management skills includes the development of personal "habits" (self-control) and problem-solving abilities (thinking). The teaching of these behaviors relies heavily on a teacher's ability to impart self-management techniques, for they help a child to respond in ways that increase the probability that he will seek positive reinforcers and avoid aversive stimuli in the future.

In teaching of personal (self-control) techniques, contingencies must be arranged that strengthen desirable work and play "habits," such as concentrating on the task at hand, working independently for reasonable periods or proceeding with a task in an orderly and systematic manner. At the heart of teaching these behaviors is the artful use of increasing and decreasing interval and ratio schedules of reinforcement.[22] A decreasing ratio reinforcement schedule can be used to teach a child to work steadily on ever-larger blocks of arithmetic problems on a single sheet of paper. At the beginning of training, he might be reinforced for doing one or two problems on a page. Shortly, he would be reinforced for doing three, then four, and so on. The rapidity with which he reaches the set goal of doing, say, six problems on a page without assistance, depends on previous training and the teacher's ability to reinforce and sustain ever-longer interactional chains.

The goal of teaching problem solving and thinking, including creative behavior, is to help a child learn how to cope with any situation — personal, social, physical, or biological — for which he does not have an immediate response that is likely to result in an appropriate reinforcer. Unfortunately, limited information from research makes problem solving a difficult subject to teach at the preschool level. Only recently has this behavior been cast in terms of observable objectives and methods of achieving them.[23] It is recognized, however, that the teaching of problem solving includes helping a child to develop a rich repertoire of abilities and knowledge; developing positive attitudes and motivations for solving problems; providing a wide variety of opportunities to engage in problem-solving behavior; giving guidance, through prompts, primes, and reinforcement support, in approaching problems and in acquiring techniques that rearrange the external environment and individual behavior (for example, concentrating and recalling) in making the solution response more probable; and withdrawing or fading guidance and support in such a way that reinforcers generate from the problem-solving behavior itself, that is, problem solving itself becomes intrinsically reinforcing. It should be apparent from this list that all preschool goals described here interrelate and augment each other.

The systematic teaching of problem solving and creative behavior as presented here is practically nonexistent in the typical preschool. Currently attempts at teaching these skills consist mainly of providing a child with unstructured situations in the hope that he can achieve these complex goals "naturally," or of merely exposing him to situations that are said to generate creativity, originality, and exploratory behavior.[24]

ESSENTIAL SUPPORTS FOR THE TEACHER

If teaching effectiveness depends on the teacher's competence in making decisions about arranging specific conditions of the educational environment so as to facilitate learning for each child, certain things are needed in order to perform the job well. A solid foundation in the technology of teaching and a working knowledge of each child are imperative. Equally important, however, are active support and assistance from aides, administrators, and, most of all, from parents. All approaches to preschool education include a program for parents that ranges from simply attending discussion groups on child rearing, to serving as teaching assistants, to acting as resource persons.

It has already been noted that parent participation in nursery school affairs is essential to ensure parent input in developing the school's philosophy of education. The mechanism for accomplishing this end is parent-teacher discussions that go beyond enumerating children's problems and beyond dwelling on family problems and possible solutions. Parent-teacher discussions should include descriptions of family practices, manners, codes of moral behavior, interests, and aspirations for the child. They should also include open discussions about family customs and the desirability of incorporating such customs, along with others, into the practices of the preschool. This frank airing of firmly held family views and coming to some consensus is one way of dealing with the current controversy over whether the value systems taught in the preschool should be those of the family, the teacher, or the administrator.

Parent participation is also needed to maximize the effect of the preschool program, particularly with respect to generalizing, elaborating, and maintaining learned behaviors.[25] For parents to be successful in extending the behaviors to the home situation, they must be willing, even at the price of some inconvenience, to arrange home conditions so that the responses required of the child resemble those he learned in school. Parents must be taught to be sensitive to the occurrences of desirable new behaviors so that they and the other members of the family will reinforce them and not just take them for granted. The best way for parents to acquire teaching techniques is through actual supervised participation in the nursery school program. A substantial by-product of this training is a simultaneous improvement in the parents' child-rearing practices that spills over to the other children in the family.

Suggestions for parent training have come from research and demonstration projects concerned with ways and means of helping parents improve child-rearing practices. In the late 1960s several field experimental studies demonstrated that mothers can readily be taught techniques to cope with their young children's conduct problems.[26] During the same period, social workers, teachers, nurses, and psychologists were exploring approaches to the direct (face-to-face) training of parents, such as the Portage Project.[27] Although the Portage Project was designed to teach parents to teach their handicapped children in their home, it proved equally suitable for training parents whose children, whether normal or deviant, attend a preschool.

Support from aides depends on their degree of competence, and their competence depends to a large extent on the objectives of the school, the methods used to achieve the objectives, and the thoroughness with which the methods are carried out. Preschools that provide more than the usual baby-sitting services make a special effort to select aides who are committed to teaching young children and who are willing and able to profit from training and supervision. In such schools aides perform more than routine housekeeping chores; they are trained to work with and to teach in accord with techniques practiced by the teacher that coincide with the philosophy of the school.

Since the teacher-child ratios in behaviorally oriented preschools are determined not only by health and safety factors but also by the personnel requirements for achieving prescribed goals for each child, these schools usually have a greater number of aides than other preschools. The hiring of more personnel raises budgetary problems, and this is a potentially serious concern if all the assistants must be full-time, paid personnel. It has been demonstrated, however, that carefully selected, properly trained, part-time volunteers serve well as teacher and aide assistants. Volunteers recruited from the ranks of high school and college students and of retired citizens constitute a teaching resource that has barely been tapped. In the past these volunteers have been relegated to child watching or to housekeeping chores. Now the whole area of training and utilizing paraprofessionals is being reassessed, particularly in light of advances in the behavioral technology of teaching.[28]

Administrators—principals, superintendents, and supervisors—play a critical role in the success or failure of a behaviorally oriented preschool program. They have, first, the responsibility for selecting teachers and, second, for seeing that teachers' efforts are adequately supported financially, professionally, and personally.

Financial support means more than providing funds for personnel, materials, equipment, and transportation. It also means providing a physical environment attuned to the behavioral objectives of the school: rooms conducive to free play, academic learning, dramatic play, music, and artistic and mechanical activities. Research is beginning to show that the physical aspect of the preschool plays a paramount role in achieving preschool goals.[29]

Administrative support for a teacher's professional growth must include the opportunity to learn more about and the freedom to institute new developments related to the behavioral approach. This requirement, comparable to maintaining quality control in business, is equally important in teaching, and it is achieved through updating practices derived from findings in applied behavior research and demonstration projects. Administrative support further presupposes responsibility for perpetuating the program. All too often promising behavior programs have been abandoned because quality control was not maintained or because new personnel were not adequately trained.

Finally, it behooves administrators to demonstrate by word and deed that the teacher's efforts are appreciated. They must reinforce even small achievements and show understanding and sympathy for occasional reactions to frustration and disappointment that inevitably accompany the demanding task of trying to help each child enjoy and profit from school to the fullest extent.

Notes

1. Patty Smith Hill, "Kindergartens of Yesterday and Tomorrow," *Journal of the National Education Association* 1 (No. 4, 1916): 294–297.

2. John B. Watson, *Psychology from the Standpoint of a Behaviorist* (Philadelphia: J. B. Lippincott Co., 1929).

3. Donald Bushell, "The Behavior Analysis Classroom," in *Early Childhood Education*, ed. Bernard Spodek (Englewood Cliffs, N.J.: Prentice-Hall, 1973), 163–175; Barbara C. Etzel *et al.*, "Experimentally Demonstrated Advantages of 'Errorless' (Programmed) Learning Procedures in Children's Learning: Assessment, Cue Relevance, Generalization, and Retention," symposium presented at the meeting of the Society for Research in Child Development, Philadelphia, March 29–April 1, 1973; Todd R. Risley, Nancy Reynolds, and Betty Hart, "The Disadvantaged: Behavior Modification with Disadvantaged Preschool Children," in *Behavior Modification: The Human Effort*, ed. R. H. Bradfield (San Rafael, Calif.: Dimensions Publishing

Co., 1970), 123–157; Carolyn L. Thomson, "Skills for Young Children," unpublished manuscript, Edna A. Hill Child Development Preschool Laboratories, Department of Human Development, University of Kansas, 1972.

4. B. Frederic Skinner, *Science and Human Behavior* (New York: Macmillan Co., 1953).

5. Carl Bereiter and Siegfried Engelmann, *Teaching the Disadvantaged Child in the Preschool* (Englewood Cliffs, N.J.: Prentice-Hall, 1966); Rupert A. Klaus and Susan W. Gray, *The Early Training Project for Disadvantaged Children: A Report after Five Years*, Monograph No. 120, *Monographs of the Society for Research in Child Development* 33 (No. 4, 1968). Marie M. Hughes, Ralph J. Wetzel, and Ronald W. Henderson, "The Tucson Early Education Model," in Spodek, *Early Childhood Education*, 230–248.

6. Lilian G. Katz, "Where Is Early Childhood Education Going?" unpublished manuscript, College of Education Curriculum Laboratory, University of Illinois, Urbana, 1973; Spodek, *Early Childhood Education*.

7. Lawrence Kohlberg and Rochelle Mayer, "Development as the Aim of Education," *Harvard Educational Review* 42 (November 1972): 449–496.

8. Erik Erikson, *Childhood and Society*, 2d ed. (New York: W. W. Norton & Co., 1963).

9. Vivian E. Todd and Helen Hefferman, *The Years before School: Guiding Preschool Children*, 2d ed. (London: Collier-Macmillan, 1970).

10. Bereiter and Engelmann, *Teaching the Disadvantaged Child in the Preschool*.

11. Spodek, *Early Childhood Education*, 69.

12. Sidney W. Bijou, *Childhood Development: The Basic Stage of Early Childhood* (Englewood Cliffs, N.J.: Prentice-Hall, 1976).

13. B. Frederic Skinner, *The Technology of Teaching* (Englewood Cliffs, N.J.: Prentice-Hall, 1968).

14. Robert A. Glaser, "A Criterion-Referenced Test," in *Criterion-Referenced Measurement: An Introduction*, ed. W. James Popham (Englewood Cliffs, N.J.: Educational Technology Publications, 1971), 41–51.

15. Thomson, "Skills for Young Children."

16. Bernard Spodek, "Staff Requirements in Early Childhood Education," in *Early Childhood Education*, ed. Ira J. Gordon, Seventy-first Yearbook of the National Society for the Study of Education, Part II (Chicago: University of Chicago Press, 1972), 347.

17. Sidney W. Bijou and Donald M. Baer, *Child Development: A Systematic and Empirical Theory*, Vol. I (Englewood Cliffs, N.J.: Prentice-Hall, 1961).

18. Lois S. Dixon, Joseph E. Spradlin, and Barbara C. Etzel, "A Study of Stimulus Control Procedures to Teach an "In-Front" Spatial Discrimination," presentation at the meeting of the Society for Research in Child Development, Philadelphia, March 29–April 1, 1973.

19. Bijou and Baer, *Child Development: A Systematic and Empirical Theory; id., Child Development: The Universal Stage of Infancy*, Vol. II (Englewood Cliffs, N.J.: Prentice-Hall, 1965).

20. Skinner, *Science and Human Behavior*; Bijou, *Child Development: Basic Stage of Early Childhood*.

21. Bijou, *Child Development: Basic Stage of Early Childhood.*

22. Bijou and Baer, *Child Development*, Vols. I and II.

23. Joseph A. Parsons, "Development and Maintenance of Arithmetic Problem-Solving Behavior in Preschool Children," unpublished dissertation, University of Illinois, Urbana-Champaign, 1973).

24. Ellis D. Evans, *Contemporary Influences in Early Childhood Education* (New York: Holt, Rinehart and Winston, 1971), Chap. 5.

25. Urie Bronfenbrenner, *Is Early Intervention Effective?* A Report on Longitudinal Evaluations of Preschool Programs, Vol. II (Washington, D.C.: U. S. Department of Health, Education, and Welfare, Office of Human Development, Office of Child Development, Children's Bureau, 1974).

26. Robert P. Hawkins *et al.*, "Behavior Theory in the Home: Amelioration of Problem Parent-Child Relations with the Parent in a Therapeutic Role," *Journal of Experimental Child Psychology* 4 (September 1966): 99–107; Saleen A. Shah, "Training and Utilizing a Mother as the Therapist for Her Child," in *Psychotherapeutic Agents: New Roles for Non-Professionals, Parents and Teachers*, ed. B. G. Guerney (New York: Holt, Rinehart and Winston, 1969), 401–407; Jane Zeilberger, Sue E. Sampen, and Howard N. Sloane, Jr., "Modification of a Child's Problem Behaviors in the Home with the Mother as Therapist," *Journal of Applied Behavior Analysis* 1 (Spring 1968): 47–53.

27. Marcia S. Shearer and David E. Shearer, "The Portage Project: A Model for Early Childhood Education," *Exceptional Children* 38 (November 1972): 210–217.

28. Teodoro Ayllon and Patricia Wright, "New Roles for the Paraprofessional," in *Behavior Modification: Issues and Extensions*, eds. Sidney W. Bijou and Emilio Ribes-Inesta (New York: Academic Press, 1972), 115–125; K. Daniel O'Leary, "The Entree of the Paraprofessional in the Classroom," *ibid.*, 93–108.

29. Lawrence A. Doke and Todd R. Risley, "The Organization of Daycare Environments: Required versus Optional Activities," *Journal of Applied Behavior Analysis* 5 (Winter 1972): 405–420; Kathryn LeLaurin and Todd R. Risley, "The Organization of Daycare Environments: Zone versus 'Man-to-Man' Staff Assignments," *ibid .*, 5 (Fall 1972): 225–232; Sandra Twardosz, Michael F. Cataldo, and Todd R. Risley, "An Open Environment Design for Infant and Toddler Daycare," *ibid.*, 7 (Winter 1974): 529–546.

10. Education and Evaluation: Cutting through the Rhetoric

Edna Shapiro

Every proposal writer knows that, if an educational program is to get financial support, the planner has to spell out the goals and objectives, as well as the means of implementation, and has to spell them out in a way that makes the program sound as if all problems have been solved in advance and all pitfalls foreseen and avoided. Furthermore, program evaluation must be built into the design. Since there is no consensus on what education for young children should be, there is an assortment of different program models, each with different aims and different strategies for achieving them. While checking on program effects seems eminently sensible and, in fact, essential, the current state of the art is severely limited both as to types of research design and range of assessment measures. It is fairly easy to evaluate how well some program aims have been realized, but it is difficult or impossible to evaluate others. The pressure to evaluate is not, however, selectively applied.

It has been said that, "Education is essentially the influence of one person on another. . . . Always the influence is that of one mind, one personality, one character on another. That, at any rate, is how it all begins."[1] Educational aims only become significant, after all, when they are transformed into programs. This can occur only in situations where real people — children, parents, teachers, principals, and all the various human contacts that make up the society of the school or preschool — are involved. Everything turns on the quality of those who put the aims, whatever they may be, into practice.

In proposal writing it is assumed that implementation will automatically be smooth, though it is obvious to anyone who has ever begun or run an educational program that this never happens, especially not at first. Funding agencies do not recognize the need to make mistakes, however essential that might be in developing a good idea or implementing a worthy aim. Because of these constraints, funding agencies, proposal writers, and evaluators are enmeshed in a web of rhetorical half-truths. It is important to recognize that it is not just programs in early childhood education that are subject to evaluation studies, not only schools that have to defend and justify their expenditures. The relatively new magazine *Evaluation* ("a forum for human service decision makers" partially funded by the National Institute of Mental Health) reports evaluation studies and critiques across a range of social programs — delivery of health care, geriatrics, criminal justice, mental health consultation, urban planning, and drug abuse, as well as education. Human services, including education, have become a commodity to be judged by commercial values. The question then becomes: Is the amount of money spent worth the resulting gain? The air is thick with promises, and the files are filled with evaluations that no one uses.

Everyone wants children to "do well." But program planners, program staff, and evaluation staff speak different languages, have different priorities, look at programs in different ways, recognize different criteria of success, and respond to different reference groups. Some evaluators seem to act as if Campbell and Stanley were always looking over their shoulders. Concern for the niceties of research design and a need to demonstrate the respectability of evaluation research preclude the use of any but conventional strategies and measures. On the one hand, there are aspirations to provide rigorous analysis and a sophisticated statistical machinery, while, on the other hand, there is an inability to deal with qualitative variables, as well as reliance on a coarse-grained assessment of program effects. No wonder so much evaluation literature is filled with model building — models that turn out to be castles in the air.

Achievement tests remain the primary assessment measure. The premise underlying the use of achievement tests in most evaluation studies is that they constitute a valid measure of intellectual development. We know which skills, facts, and concepts must be acquired, in what order, by what time. Then we drop in our lines to fish out the facts and concepts, and depending on the catch, place each child on a scale indicating how far ahead or behind he or she is in terms of chronological age months or grade months or percentiles or stanines, and how far ahead or behind the child will be in three or five years.

The approach to measurement is marked by an obsession with timing and rate of acquisition; the approach to teaching is marked by profound distrust of the processes of learning and an assumption that learning cannot occur without formidable effort and considerable suffering.

Part of the problem lies in the lackluster quality of education in so many of the nation's schools. There is a mutual support system: dull evaluation studies to fit dull educational programs. Many teachers and administrators seem to be cowed by the apparatus, apparent objectivity, and technical jargon of the testing establishment. Educational programs are shaped to fit the contour of the evaluation. Hundreds of classroom hours are spent on worksheets intended to help children master a skill that will aid them on the achievement test. Evaluators press program designers to operationalize their objectives. It sounds like a good idea, but the process often develops a momentum of its own and leads to reducing concepts and goals to miniscule bits of behavior. (In order to increase a child's sense of self-esteem, for example, the teacher is enjoined to remember each child's name and nationality.) The result is a kind of miniaturization of competence, and a debasement of teaching.

MEASUREMENT GOALS

The evaluators' ecological niche has been the desk, the computer room, and the professional meeting, where issues of design, sampling, and regression analysis are primary. It might be helpful if evaluators became more familiar with classrooms and schools. When visiting programs intended for young children, one often wonders how much of what one sees and what the director, teachers, aides, and parents say about the program will actually get into the computer and the final report.

Take a Head Start center in a small town in the Southeast: a pleasant frame building on a large grassy lot; aged trees, perfect for climbing; a vegetable garden tended by the children. The rooms are light and airy and house standard preschool equipment. There are plentiful though conventional paintings and collages; the curriculum is undistinguished, except for recent efforts to build connections with the children's background culture. Children are bused to the center, but the trips are relatively short, about twenty minutes.

Before Head Start, many, if not most, of the children were completely homebound. Except for occasional ceremonial visits, the only people they knew and talked with were members of their immediate family. Even when families are large, that is a restricted range of social contact. The child's first exposure to unfamiliar adults and children came when they reached the age of six and went to school, and, for many of them, the language spoken at school was different from that at home.

What parents and teachers see as the central contribution of Head Start in this community is the opportunity it provides for the children to play with other children and to talk with other children and adults, to learn to function in a group. The benefits of Head Start are perceived to focus on social interaction, the opportunity for verbal interchange, and an exposure to a variety of people (apart from health care and parent participation). The elementary school staff say that they can tell which children have been in the Head Start program: they make an easier transition into kindergarten, they know more, and they are more verbal and outgoing. But this is all soft data or hearsay; it is not easily quantified. Although social interaction is one of the goals of Head Start, formal evaluations, by and large, have been concerned with the presence or absence of "cognitive gains." Cognitive gains almost certainly take place as a result of the children's experiences, but they are more in the nature of broadening horizons and changing the orientation of the self in relation to other people. Such learning cannot be directly measured by existing academic yardsticks.

In one of the pueblos near Albuquerque I visit a family consisting of a mother, father, and three children. Danny, the youngest, is almost two, and he is in Phyllis Levenstein's Verbal Interaction Program. A young man comes to visit Danny, brings him a book, reads it to him, and leaves the book. The mother likes the program. The young man works up the road and passes the house on his way to and from work, and Danny runs to the window and calls, "Hi, George." Danny's mother feels that the program "gives Danny someone new to know, someone outside the family . . . . And then the older children ask Danny, 'Did George come today?' 'What did he bring you?' . . . And they read the book too." It is true that the book, the home visitor, and the program do promote verbal interaction, but not quite in the way the program description or the evaluation reports read.

Take another example: a very successful behavioristic Follow-Through program in the primary grades. The evaluation reports state that the program has "reversed academic failure" and that the majority of the children involved are performing at or above grade level on first-, second-, and third-grade achievement tests. The school administration is enthusiastic about the program, and the reports indicate parental support and approval. Almost all of the parents with whom we spoke, however, rather nervously voiced complaints: "My daughter used to love school, now she weeps, sometimes she throws up, she has to be forced to go to school. When I went to talk to the teachers—oh, I've talked with everyone there—[the teacher] says, 'I don't have time to give individual attention . . . .' I work in the program so I really shouldn't say anything, but I think it's too much for the young children. Maybe for the older ones . . . . My husband noticed how nervous Jim was when he started school. Now I'm worried about the next one, because Jim is easygoing, but Roger is . . . different." Another parent says, "Oh, they learn to do their numbers, but you have to ask them exactly the way they learned it. If you use any other words [my daughter] doesn't know what you are talking about. And they [teachers] shout, they scream at the children. And the children come home and scream. I say, 'Don't yell.' And she says, 'That's the way the teacher does.'"

I went to a session in an elementary school where a representative of a major testing concern "explained" the results of the fall testing program to the school's teachers, kindergarten through third grade. The teachers all came, bringing packets that gave the scores of the children in their classes. The scores were reported in the kind of detail that only a machine technology can provide—grade equivalents, percentiles, stanines, and plotted to show growth curves; and, for each child, the correct or incorrect response to each item on each subtest. It was apparent, however, that the teachers did not understand the complicated data sheets they had been given. They did not know what to make of the fact that their children were below grade level when the testing had been done in the second week after school started, they did not know whether they should be focusing on grade equivalents or percen-

tiles, and they did not know what stanines were. Nor did they know
what relation all these facts had to one another. The testing company
representative explained that the scores were not to be taken too seriously. He talked about measurement error and pointed out that some
children might not have been feeling good that day, maybe some kid's
mother and father had had an argument just before school, or some
girl might have been worried about her sick pet and therefore might
not have given her full attention to the test questions. I was confused.
Here was a man whose professional identity and livelihood were tied to
mass testing, and, after explaining the intricacies of the measures to a baf-
fled audience, he went on to apologize for the inadequacies of the tests.

He warned the teachers not to take the grade-equivalent score too
seriously. Nor were they to study correct and incorrect scores of individual students on the subtests because they then might think that the
children really knew the answers to the questions they got right and
did not know the answers to the ones they got wrong, which could be
misleading information. The one datum that he personally felt was
meaningful and could be useful to them was the growth curve. Since
no one understood what that meant, he plotted it out on a blackboard
and explained that the growth curve offered a prediction of how the
child would do in succeeding years, on succeeding tests.

The best I could make of it all was: you cannot trust the individual
items; you cannot trust the normative data, that is, the grade-equivalent scores. If you put it all together, however, you can, by some leger-
demain, predict just how well a child will do two, four, or six years
from now.

STANDARDIZATION

There is something anomalous in the fact that professional people
think that they should put more credence in the results of a forty-five-
minute test than in the synthesis of knowledge and impressions gained
in day-to-day, yearlong contact with a child. It suggests the extent to
which people have been browbeaten by notions of scientific objectivity, mass norms, and the cult of testing expertise. Lack of faith in one's
own perceptions and ideas also hampers the ability to develop individual curricula. So many teachers of young children have lost faith in
their power to invent, to know what children will be interested in, and
to decide what it is important to know. Tests seep into early childhood

programs in the form of prepackaged curricula designed to lead to higher scores on achievement tests. Thus, from the age of three or four, children in many schools spend much of their time with work-sheets—shaping letters and numbers, filling in blanks, circling right answers, drawing lines to show what goes with what. This means that for three, four, or five years they are getting more or less the same school curriculum: drill on numbers, letters, colors, initial sounds, simple concepts. Indeed, many kindergarten teachers have complained that children in Head Start have already "had" the kindergarten curriculum and that there is nothing for them to do.

It is appalling that there could be such a narrow definition of what it is important to know and of what it is useful and interesting for young children to learn. This narrowing is, I believe, directly attributable to the limited kinds of information that tests have asked for; or, perhaps it is more accurate to say that the narrowing is a result of teachers' and administrators' conceptions of what the tests are asking for.

It is odd that, with all the accumulated sophistication about test construction, the tests themselves are remarkably poorly designed. Instructions are often confusing and excessively wordy. What is being tested may turn out to be an understanding of item format, which is, of course, a prerequisite to a correct response. Review of standardized achievement and reading readiness tests currently used for kindergarten and elementary schoolchildren indicates that "the present crop of standardized measures are often designed much more for administrative ease than for examinee appropriateness."[2] The content is patently unrelated to anything except test-constructors' ideas of what it is possible to illustrate pictorially and easy to score. Vocabulary tests often demand specialized and culture-specific knowledge. In a vocabulary test, selection is inevitably arbitrary, but each word is presumed to represent a set of words of established frequency, and the score is presumed to represent the child's vocabulary range. If this is so, why are kindergarten children and first graders across the country expected to know such words as orchestra, trapeze, steeple, foliage, aquarium, toboggan . . .?

Analysis of the capacities presumably being tapped by different items shows that items supposed to measure one function, for example, reading comprehension, require a range of auxiliary skills in information processing for their correct solution. Consider this item from a "popular" reading readiness test:[3]

Look at the pictures in row 4. Listen carefully: This is a story about three living things you might find around a farm. One day they were talking about how they liked to live. One said, "I like fresh air. When I was very little, I lived in a nest in an apple tree. I lived outside all the time." Another one said, "I like to live outside, too. I lived in a nest when I was very little, but it was on the ground." The other one said, "I don't like it outside very well. I like to live in barns and houses." Find which one spoke *first* and fill in the oval under it. [Note: the three pictures are a mouse or rat, a rabbit, and a bird.]

This item is offensive in its condescending anthropomorphism and the misinformation it conveys, but what is even worse is the fact that analysis of this item shows, as Stephen Klein points out, "that it requires the pupil to store fourteen separate units of information, plus sequence, and inferences drawn from the information."[4]

PROGRAM GOALS

How can we bring the rhetoric and reality of program evaluation closer to those of the program? The more conventional way of accomplishing this has been to call for the specification of goals and objectives as an essential first step both in developing programs and in devising appropriate evaluation instruments. In programs with carefully articulated behavioral objectives, the target behaviors are fairly easy to evaluate. Some of the unintended side effects may not, however, be so easy to assess. It has been suggested for years that educational programs have to be looked at as coherent systems and that techniques designed to promote particular goals, for example, developing cognitive competence, have to be assessed in terms of a system of goals, not merely in terms of a single goal in isolation from others.[5] When discussing interrelations between psychological theory and educational ideology, Margery Franklin and Barbara Biber have pointed to the importance of looking at the side effects of programs, especially those based on behavioristic psychology that usually make use of behavior-modification techniques: "In our view, children in such classrooms are not only learning the specific skills and modes of conduct which are the 'target behaviors' of the program, but are inevitably picking up other messages, learning other things, as well. [Among these are that] one works or behaves properly in order to achieve external rewards, at first tangible rewards like candy and/or the privilege of playing with a favorite toy or engaging in a preferred activity, and perhaps subsequently (if training is successful) to receive praise from some momentarily benevolent authority figure."[6]

Looking at the problem of side effects from a different point of view, Michael Scriven, one of the most influential figures in current thinking about educational evaluation, found that close analysis of the extent to which program goals were met did not adequately cover program effects. As a result, he suggested that the unintended effects of programs should be given at least the same weight as the intended effects, and he developed the notion of "goal-free evaluation": "The less the external evaluator hears about the goals of the project, the less tunnel vision will develop, the more attention will be paid to *looking* for *actual* effects (rather than *checking* on *alleged* effects)."[7] We witness the birth of a new rhetoric. In effect, what Scriven says is, do not look at what they say, just look at what they do.

Scriven's suggestion takes us through the looking glass to where goals and side effects have a kind of Tweedledum and Tweedledee partnership. It may be that excessive focus on stated goals can blind program implementers and evaluators to other things. But the rationale does matter, and both implementation and evaluation have to connect with goals. Certainly a goal-free orientation, to use Scriven's term, would be easier than following the directive to take a whole roster of different educational goals into account in designing an evaluation strategy.

EVALUATION ON A NATIONAL SCALE

Evaluation of the Planned Variation programs of Head Start and Follow-Through follows the directive of being all things to all programs. These evaluations clearly point up most of the problems that beset this kind of large-scale effort to assess the comparative effectiveness of different educational approaches. The concept (education as experimentation) is grand; the design (a carefully worked out longitudinal study of at least seven years' duration) is ambitious; the range of variation among sponsors (from Engelmann-Becker to Bank Street and the Educational Development Center) is broad.[8]

And the problems have turned out to be insurmountable. Sponsors' sites are located in different geographic regions, and the groups of children in each are of different sizes and ethnic composition. Since the program operates only in certain schools within any district, tracking the subjects becomes a formidable task; it has been difficult, often impossible, to find comparison groups from a similar socioeconomic background who are not in other intervention programs. Thus, comparisons among sponsors are confounded by urban-rural and ethnic differences, while comparison of children in Follow-Through with those not in Follow-Through is often a test of unplanned variation.

The scale of the evaluation is difficult for the mind to grasp. For instance, Garry McDaniels reports that "ten tons of materials and 2,200 people in the field were needed for a scaled-down effort in the spring of 1972." The cost is also staggering. The original plan to collect complete data on five cohorts had to be cut back. It was estimated, McDaniels notes, that if all possible data were collected on the five cohorts, the cost would be close to forty million dollars.[9]

Massive amounts of data have been collected, analyzed, transformed into multiple regression equations, and put through the analysis of covariance. Methodological issues — how missing data have been dealt with, how the analysis of covariance was handled — are spelled out in detail, and statistical formulas are presented that are unintelligible to any but the statistically sophisticated. Explanation of conventions adopted, definition of terms, justification of statistical procedures are always necessary. The detail as well as the language makes it clear that these reports are constructed by evaluators and statisticians for other evaluators and statisticians.

The problems involved in mounting an evaluation of such scope are indeed enormously complex and require an analytic model that can cope with comparisons of Follow-Through and non-Follow-Through programs, of sponsors, of the effects of socioeconomic status, of city size, and of attendance, of one-, two-, three-, and four-year effects, as well as determining the stability of effects over time and in relation to grade level. But when you come right down to a fulcrum on which to balance this elaborate structure, what is there but the old standard achievement test data? What gets lost in all of the equations and tables is the fact that the core of assessment is, for Follow-Through, primarily the Metropolitan Achievement Test and some additional measures like the Gumpgookies; for Head Start, it is the Preschool Inventory, the Stanford-Binet, and the New York University Achievements Tests (assessing knowledge of letters, numerals, shape names, premath and prescience concepts, and prepositions), and the Motor Inhibition Test.

In spite of the drawbacks, there are hopeful signs. The fact that parents' and teachers' responses to the program were collected is an indication that such attitudes and feelings were considered relevant. A chapter on program implementation that describes some of the problems that sponsors had in setting up programs at some of the sites provides formal recognition that programs are not created by fiat. These qualitative reports do not, for the most part, enter into the hard data of the comparative study. The fact that they are included suggests that it is no longer possible to ignore such variables.

Some auxiliary studies of Head Start Planned Variation show that we have come a long way from the Westinghouse Report in which Head Start was treated almost as a presence-absence variable (year-long, summer program, none). While the primary focus of the Planned Variation design has been on comparison of models, the inevitable variation within programs under the auspices of the same sponsor has resulted in attempts to measure the extent to which the variations still can be considered to match the models. Assessing the "extent of implementation" is now seen as a necessary bridge between program description and outcome, and, in itself, gives rise to interesting and frustrating research issues. What is full implementation? How much variation can be tolerated among classrooms presumably exemplifying the same model? Should all departures from model specification be given equal weight? In the more behavioristic models behavioral objectives are specified more clearly and more definitely. In more comprehensive models objectives and desirable teacher behavior are based on more general principles, and adaptation to individual circumstances is encouraged. The more prescriptive models are, therefore, easier to assess.[10]

After Head Start models had been implemented in different communities for several years, the Office of Child Development commissioned the Huron Institute to study the residual effects of the models. The question of how and in what ways models survive the departure of the sponsor is of obvious practical concern. The Huron study found that in some sites many components of the Head Start models did persist; in others, site staff "talked as if they were still using the model in every way," but the Huron staff did not see it. (This raises some interesting questions about teachers' reports of what they are doing in their classrooms.) Sponsors and models are an important focus for future study since, as Anne Monaghan points out, "Sponsors will continue to affect greater and greater numbers of teachers and children . . . .

Therefore, educational innovations should consider their effects not only on the 'target population' receiving service for a limited period of time, but should also track the development of those delivering that service. In the case of HSPV, the true target population may have been sponsors and models."[11]

But the fact is that the focus was on outcome measures, on how the children performed on achievement tests. How does the evaluation take account of how well tests fit particular programs? I have argued elsewhere that children in conventional schoolrooms learn—as an intended or an unintended effect—a set of skills that are more in line with the skills necessary for doing well on achievement tests than do children in more open classrooms.[12] Aside from interminable drill on the skills themselves, they learn to look to the teacher as rule maker, to accept what the teacher tells them with little question, and to do what they are asked. Children become accustomed to a question-and-answer format and to the notion that every question has a correct answer. The more behavioristic the program, the greater the focus on acquiring skills that feed directly into achievement test taking. So it should come as no surprise that the models with the strongest showing, where the Follow-Through children did significantly better than the comparison group, were the Engelmann-Becker and the Behavior Analysis models (with High-Scope and Individualized Early Learning coming up second); better, that is, on the Metropolitan Achievement Test and the Wide Range Achievement Test. The finding that highly structured models emphasizing short-term achievement lead to higher achievement scores should cause us to sigh with relief. If *they* did not lead to higher achievement scores, things would be even worse than we thought.

But what about the less structured programs, the sponsors who are trying for a wider range of goals over a more extended span of time? It is generally agreed that these measures cannot provide adequate indexes of their impact.

It is encouraging that some studies are now looking at ways in which different kinds of children respond to different kinds of programs,[13] but to my knowledge these studies have been limited to analysis of distal variables of high socioeconomic status, low initial scores, and gains on the Preschool Inventory and the Stanford-Binet. It will be a while before we have a clear understanding of how to match programs and children, and, perhaps more important, know how to build in flexibility so that programs can adapt to changes in children's functioning.

NEW VIEWS ON EVALUATION

Many critics of educational evaluation, as currently conceived and practiced, have pointed to the need for a more precise analysis of educational situations, for techniques that document what goes on in classrooms, and for detailed study of educational transactions. No one recommends throwing out the whole concept of evaluating educational programs. Indeed, there is a practical as well as a moral imperative to determine the extent to which programs do what they say they will do, and also to check on their unintended effects. Although standard tests are mandated in many states, the way they are interpreted and reported (to teachers, parents, and children) is up to individual school administrators. It is important that those who teach and direct programs become more aware of their options. There are different kinds of evaluative techniques, and school people can and should have a say in the kinds of procedures that are used to judge what is going on in their classrooms and schools.

It is perhaps not surprising that much of the impetus for finding different, less conventional, less test-centered methods of evaluating programs has come from school people who have been identified with more open, program-centered, and informal approaches to education. Much grumbling about the sterility of conventional methods has come from those who have chafed at the circumscribed definition of accomplishment and felt that their programs were misrepresented by the needle's-eye view of competence defined by achievement tests.

Some administrators and teachers have been experimenting with different ways of evaluating their programs by observing and recording what goes on, what individual children do, and how different children make use of the opportunities offered in a classroom that has a heterogeneous program, by keeping logs and diaries, and by using children's work as a way of assessing what they have learned and in what areas they need help.[14]

Teachers and school administrators should try out some of these ideas. Other techniques, for example, Educational Testing Service's new CIRCUS battery and the Cincinnati Autonomy Test Battery (CATB), try for a broader range of assessment than the conventional paper-and-pencil achievement and intelligence tests.[15] But these newer methods, like the old standbys, should be labeled "for experimental purposes only." They have not solved the problems. If a teacher uses, say, Banta's Dog and Bone Test, and is surprised that some children do not "generate alternative solutions to problems" as readily as she had thought they would, the teacher should not necessarily assume that the test is right and she is wrong. The discrepancy can be a source of learning and self-examination for the teacher and lead to sharper, more careful observation of the children. Teachers can profit from using corrective devices to test against their own perceptions of what is happening in their classrooms (as noted in the Huron Institute study, mentioned above.) Teachers can pair up and observe in each other's classrooms, trying out different observation guides and mapping their own and the children's behavior and interactions. In short, it is necessary to be inventive.

It is also necessary for teachers to become more knowledgeable about the limitations of standard testing so that they are not overawed by normative data and so that they acquire or regain confidence in their perceptions of and reactions to what children do and say in their classrooms. Such suggestions are, of course, a sad reflection of the state of the art of evaluation today. It may seem like advocating hand tools in a machine age, a rebirth perhaps akin to baking bread at home and quilting. Indeed, teachers in at least some of the nursery schools of the twenties always carried a notebook and pencil to set down a telling observation.[16] In addition to providing information about individual children and their relations to each other and the teacher, this kind of documentation places the teacher in a strategic position. She is no longer the docile recipient of incomprehensible data. She becomes a participant in the process of assessment. She will notice that young children can and do pay attention and even sit still for long periods of time when they are interested, that young children have a lot of information about local geography, television programs, rhymes, films, songs, sports, the rules of games. Some will have a fund of plant or animal lore. Some may know about birth and sex, about death and illness; others may know about vitamins, about male chauvinism, about karate, about racism, about shoplifting, about religious ceremonies, or about hunger. Some may also have inaccurate information and misconceptions about things they know something about.

Could we make the radical assumption that, given a moderately enriched environment, moderately encouraging and flexible teachers, and moderately interesting materials, children with average endowment would also learn the fundamentals of how to read and write, add and subtract, the names of colors, the common geometric forms, and how to refer to relationships of position in space and time?

The fundamental contribution of Michael Cole, John Gay, Joseph Glick, and Donald Sharp in studying the cultural context of thinking is, I believe, their insistence that the group they studied, the Kpelle, being human, must be capable of thinking — of remembering, classifying, and dealing with abstractions. If their subjects did not do well, they reasoned that the fault must lie in the task or the instructions, not in the capacity of the subjects.[17]

Could we not apply this to the children in our schools today? If some of the lockstep of the age-graded curriculum geared to age-graded achievement tests were relaxed, perhaps children and teachers would find schools more lively and challenging places to spend their time. Perhaps they would not learn just to read but to enjoy reading, not just to compute but to play mathematical games, not just to answer but to ask questions. What a challenge to evaluation such competence would be.

Notes

1. John F. Wolfenden, in C. H. Dobinson, *Education in a Changing World* (New York: Oxford University Press, 1951), 47.

2. Stephen P. Klein, "The Uses and Limitations of Standardized Tests in Meeting the Demands for Accountability," *Evaluation Comment* 2 (January 1971): 1–7.

3. The source of this item, and of the preceding vocabulary items, is not given because, following Klein's approach, the intent is not to criticize any particular test, but the genre.

4. Klein, "Uses and Limitations of Standardized Tests." 4.

5. Barbara Biber, Edna Shapiro, and David Wickens, *Promoting Cognitive Growth: A Developmental-Interaction Point of View* (Washington, D.C.: National Association for the Education of Young Children, 1971).

6. Margery. B. Franklin and Barbara Biber, "Psychological Perspectives and Early Childhood Education: Some Relations between Theory and Practice," in *Current Topics in Early Children Education*, Vol. I, ed. Lilian G. Katz (Hillsdale, N.J.: Lawrence Erlbaum, 1976).

7. Michael Scriven, "Prose and Cons about Goal-Free Evaluation," *Evaluation Comment* 3 (December 1972): 1–4; reprinted in *Evaluation in Education: Current Applications*, ed. W. James Popham (Berkeley, Calif.: McCutchan Publishing Corporation, 1974), 34–43.

8. Final reports are not expected until 1978; these remarks are, therefore, based on interim reports. It may be worth noting that the reports run to several hundred mimeographed pages each. The ten program sponsors being assessed are: Far West Laboratory, Responsive Education; University of Arizona, Tucson Early Education Model; Bank Street College; University of Oregon, Engelmann-Becker; University of

Kansas, Behavior Analysis; High/Scope, Cognitively Oriented Curriculum; University of Florida, Parent Education; Educational Development Center, Open Education; University of Pittsburgh, Individualized Early Learning; Southwest Education Development Laboratory, Bilingual Education. The first Follow-Through group entered kindergarten in 1969–70, and the original plan was to study five successive cohorts. See Marvin G. Cline *et al.*, *Education as Experimentation: Evaluation of the Follow Through Planned Variation Model*. Vol. IIA *Two Year Effects of Follow Through;* Vol. IIB. *Monographs and Appendices* (Cambridge, Mass.: Abt Associates, 1975).

9. Garry L. McDaniels, "The Evaluation of Follow Through," *Educational Leadership* 33 (December 1975): 7–11.

10. Carol Van Deusen Lukas, "Measuring the Extent of Treatment Implementation," paper presented at meetings of the American Psychological Association, New Orleans, La., August 1974.

11. Anne Coolidge Monaghan, "HSVP in Retrospect," paper presented at meetings of the American Psychological Association, New Orleans, La., 1974. Emphasis in the original.

12. Edna Shapiro, "Educational Evaluation: Rethinking the Criteria of Competence," *School Review* 81 (August 1973): 523–549.

13. See Helen J. Featherstone, "Child Characteristics by Model Interactions," paper presented at meetings of the American Psychological Association, New Orleans, La., August 1974.

14. For examples of some of these techniques, see Gene R. Hawes, "Managing Open Education: Testing, Evaluation and Accountability," *Nation's Schools* 93 (1974): 33–47; and *Testing and Evaluation: New Views*, ed. Vito Perrone, Monroe D. Cohen, and Lucy Prete Martin (Washington, D.C.: Association of Childhood Education International, 1975).

15. CIRCUS: *Comprehensive Program of Assessment Services for Pre-primary Children*, manual and technical report — preliminary version, 1974 (Princeton, N.J.: Educational Testing Service, 1974); Thomas J. Banta, "Tests for the Evaluation of Early Childhood Education: The Cincinnati Autonomy Test Battery (CATB)," in *Cognitive Studies*, Vol. I, ed. Jerome Hellmuth (New York: Brunner/Mazel, 1970), 424–490.

16. Harriet M. Johnson, *Children in the Nursery School* (New York: John Day Company, 1928; reissued by Agathon Press, New York, in 1972).

17. Michael Cole, John Gay, Joseph A. Glick, and Donald W. Sharp, *The Cultural Context of Learning and Thinking* (New York: Basic Books, 1971).

11. The Socialization of Teachers for Early Childhood Programs

Lilian G. Katz

A teacher "should have a fair education. By this I mean she should have a doctor's degree in psychology and medicine. Sociology as a background is advisable. She should be an experienced carpenter, mason, mechanic, plumber and a thoroughly trained musician and poet. At least five years' practical experience in each of these branches is essential. Now at eighty-three, she is ready!"[1] A more current listing of the ideal qualifications for teachers for early childhood programs might also include anthropology, linguistics, ethnic studies, and ecology. One further modification, which reflects the contemporary desire to encourage men to become teachers of young children, would be to end the exclusive use of the feminine gender.

In spite of the complex nature of the above description, most states have set forth few formal requirements for those who teach our youngest children. The issues surrounding such requirements are many and complex. They reflect a variety of conceptual and practical problems, as well as ideological, economic, and political issues, and it is the specific purpose of this chapter to point out selected issues in the conceptualization, design, and implementation of programs intended to prepare teachers of young children, with particular emphasis on the special problems of those who intend to teach in the preschool setting.

TEACHER EDUCATION AS SOCIALIZATION

The general term "socialization" has been defined as "the process by which persons acquire the knowledge, skills, and dispositions that make them more or less able members of their society."[2] The concept of socialization alerts people to other useful goals and processes. Teacher education is a more specific instance of occupational or professional socialization. It includes the dimensions indicated in this definition, but specifies the group into which the individual is being socialized. As W. E. Moore defines it, professional socialization "involves acquiring the requisite knowledge and also the sense of occupational norms typical of the fully qualified practitioner."[3] The concept of occupational socialization should serve to enlarge the range and type, as well as relative emphases, of variables to be considered when thinking about teacher education. Thinking about teacher education simply as a type of training program tends to overemphasize skill acquisition at the expense of occupational norms. Thinking about teacher education as an educational program, on the other hand, may stress the acquisition of knowledge and neglect both skill acquisition and the internalization of occupational norms. Such relative emphases are not inherent in concepts of training or of education.

Using the concept of occupational socialization, teacher education can be defined as sets of activities (and actions) that are intended to help candidates acquire the requisite knowledge, skills, habits, values, dispositions, and norms that enable them to enter the occupation of teaching. The activities that constitute teacher education are numerous and varied. They can include, for example, courses, field trips, lectures, practicums, modules, microteaching, observations of children, independent reading, and a host of other activities. There are many ways in which these activities may vary. This chapter suggests the kinds of variables that might affect teacher education.

VARIABLES RELATED TO TEACHER EDUCATION PROGRAMS

Broad categories or classes of variables impinge upon the sets of activities, actions, and processes that constitute a teacher education program. Experience suggests that the variables are complex, interacting, and confounding factors that are separated here only to facilitate discussion and inquiry. They have not yet been assigned an order of importance; nor is their relative impact on the activities or outcomes of teacher education known at this time. Eight classes of variables are listed and defined briefly below. In succeeding pages these classes of variables are considered more specifically as they relate to early childhood teacher education programs.

Goals and their assessment — These are the general and specific outcomes that the activities and actions constituting teacher education programs are intended to achieve and methods of assessing those outcomes.

Candidates — Whether they are trainees, students, or recruits, candidates vary as to age, sex, socioeconomic background, motivation, intelligence, creativity, and many other characteristics.

Staff participants — Again, there is variation in age, experience, ideology, skill, knowledge, and other aspects. Some staff members are senior professors; some are graduate assistants; some are cooperating teachers in public schools; some are directors of day-care centers.

Program content — A variety of facts, information, theories, knowledge, ideas, skills, and techniques are transmitted to candidates via the activities and actions within a teacher education program.

Time — How long a program lasts (one, two, or four years) and the timing and sequencing or temporal order and simultaneity of activities presented to the candidates are also important considerations.

Ethos — There are ways in which the social and intellectual climate or atmosphere of the socialization setting may vary. Certainly the ethos of the setting is reflected in the affective tone and intellectual content of interpersonal relationships among and between candidates and staff members.

Location and setting — The teacher education program may be located at or part of a conventional college campus, an urban commuter campus, a teachers' center, a community college, a school district, a demonstration project, or a campus laboratory school, and there are even more possibilities.

Regulation — Certification requirements are set by the state, and the federal government may exercise control through funding agencies. School districts, legislatures at both the state and federal levels, and government bureaus also can function as regulatory forces. Finally, there are intrainstitutional regulations and requirements, as well as the activities of political action and pressure groups.

EDUCATION PROGRAMS FOR TEACHERS OF YOUNG CHILDREN

Goals and Their Assessment

If this chapter had been prepared prior to the 1960s, the term "nursery school" might well have appeared in the title. Since the era of large-scale intervention programs like Head Start, nursery school as a term has gradually dropped from use and been replaced by "preschool" or "early childhood education." It would appear that preschool encompasses more fully the varied age groups and types of settings served by such programs. As for early childhood education, it usually encompasses all programs and classes for children up to and including the age of eight.

In conjunction with changes in program terminology, there has been some reluctance to use the term "teacher," especially in discussions of day-care center staffing. Terms like "child care worker," and "care giver," are increasingly being used, and the federally initiated training program developed by the Office of Child Development in the Department of Health, Education, and Welfare adopted the term "child development associate" for adults working in Head Start and other preschool settings.

Why there is this reluctance to use the term "teacher" is not entirely clear. Perhaps it is an association of the term with conventional state teaching credentials, whereas many adults working in early childhood programs have paraprofessional or assistant status. It may also reflect the negative sentiments of many workers in programs like Head Start and other community-based early childhood centers toward teachers in conventional public schools. Or, it may be that, to a large extent, the reluctance to use the term teacher stems from complexities in conceptualizing the adult's role and functions in programs for very young children. Some of these complexities can be seen in a statement made by Edward Zigler when he was director of the Office of Child Development at the time that he introduced the Child Development Associate (CDA) project:

The central element determining whether a child care program is developmental or not will be the quality of the child's educator . . . that is the quality of the adult who takes primary responsibility for the development and socialization of the child. If we do not have an adequate number of such individuals equipped to take on this developmental role, then I think we will be assigning our children in ever larger numbers, to the type of care that is deleterious to their growth and development.[4]

In the passage cited above, the adult role is referred to as being the child's educator. But the responsibilities include development, socialization, growth, and care. These multiple and overlapping responsibilities may have been generally understood or taken for granted in the conceptualization of the older nursery school teacher, as implied by the quotation that opened this chapter. Expansion and development of the field in the last dozen or more years seem to have undermined that traditional consensus and understanding. Presumably newer terms (for example, day-care worker, care giver, CDA) serve to remind us of the wide range of functions that adults in preschool settings are expected to fulfill. For the purposes of this chapter, however, the term "teacher" is preferred.

The wide range of the functions performed by preschool teachers gives rise to more than terminological problems. It seems that there is a lack of agreement concerning what constitutes "good" or even "adequate" teaching. There has been extensive effort, through curriculum model development (for example, Planned Variation in Head Start), to emphasize preferred teaching procedures and objectives during the past decade, but the effort seems to have provoked bitter divergence among workers in the field over the functions of teachers of young children.[5] It is unlikely that Piagetians and behavior analysts would characterize "effective" or even "adequate" teaching in the same way. Just among Piagetians, themselves, several pedagogical controversies remain unresolved.

Six basic competence areas and nine "personal capacities" have been outlined as the goals of the CDA teacher-training program.[6] Methods for transforming the goals into the sets of activities that constitute a training program are not, however, clear as yet. The main thrust of the CDA Project is to provide a credential that trainees earn "by *demonstrating competence* to work with preschool children in the performance or competency-based programs."[7] As with other teacher education programs in the performance or competency-based mode, the CDA credential is based on "actual performance with children."[8] Even though certain "personal capacities" are labeled "essential," the performance orientation implies strong emphasis on acquiring a repertoire of demonstrable skills and techniques.

In order to formulate the goals of a socialization process, it is useful to identify specific segments of the occupation. Four interrelated segments that encompass the functions, attributes, and behaviors (that is, program goals) into which students are to be socialized are outlined briefly below:

Role definition — Functions, duties, responsibilities, and obligations assigned to and expected of those holding teaching positions. To some extent the role definition for a day-care center teacher is different from that of the nursery school or kindergarten teacher who works only half days or perhaps three mornings a week. The day-care teacher's role is likely to encompass a wider range of functions and duties than that of the nursery school teacher. As for early childhood programs, the functions of the teachers are likely to vary with the age of pupils: the younger the child, the wider the range of the child's functions for which the adult must assume responsibility.

Teaching style — Style refers to individual and distinctive ways of enacting the role of teacher. Two teachers may accept the same role definition, but differ in the way in which the role is rendered. These variations are sometimes labeled personality traits or attitudes. Examples of style variables are warmth, friendliness, patience, enthusiasm, seriousness, and so on. When we make the statement that a program "depends on the personality of the teacher," we are very likely referring to style variations in teachers. Teachers in the Becker-Engelmann model, to take one example, all share a common role definition, but individual teachers perform those same functions with more or less warmth and humor, as well as variations in tempo.

Skills and techniques — Skills and techniques have been defined by E. K. Beller as the strategies by which teachers expect to accomplish their objectives.[9] The skills and techniques or competencies refer to behaviors displayed "on the job," while working with children and parents (storyreading, engaging children in movement or dance, behavior modification, engaging children in conversations, teaching phonics, and the like). The underlying knowledge bases are implied in this segment.

Professional or occupational identification — This segment is represented by a cluster of variables, such as occupational norms, attitudes toward clients and colleagues, teachers' ethics, ideological commitment, and professional self-image.

When the sets of activities provided for candidates focus heavily on the acquisition of skills and techniques, they constitute a training program; when they focus on the underlying knowledge base or on information about the knowledge base, then the program can be described as teacher education. If teacher education is to be a process of socialization into an occupation (ideally, a profession), then the sets of activities must include goals and assessments in all four segments outlined above, but the optimum proportion of time or effort to be assigned to goals and assessment of each of the segments is not clear. A candidate who has a clear role definition but lacks adequate skills is not likely to be very effective in the day-care center. Similarly, a candidate with a strong ideological commitment but an insufficient repertoire of skills and techniques is likely to flounder in practice. The regular assessment of a candidate's progress with respect to goals in each segment may serve to ascertain the optimum proportions of time and effort assigned to respective segments.

The discussion and controversy surrounding competency-based teacher education seem to have stimulated new sensitivity to the goals of teacher education among early childhood specialists. One problem is the extent to which competency-based teacher education leads to a reductionist conception of the nature of teaching.[10] The pressure to specify "demonstrable skills" could, although it does not necessarily have to, result in the formulation of long lists of discrete skills, each of which can be observed and assessed separately. This approach to the goals of the program and to the assessment of candidates implies that teaching is an aggregate of separable skills. Indeed, much research on teacher behavior suffers from this weakness.

While the teaching of young children includes sets of demonstrable skills, it is better to think of teaching in terms of larger patterns of behaviors, including the ability to decide which skills to use and when to use them. Competency-based programs seem to differ from conventional teacher education primarily in terms of both explicitness and specificity of goals and objectives. Perhaps the effectiveness of a teacher resides not in behavior per se, but in the meaning the learner assigns to that behavior. Discrete episodes of teaching derive their meaning from the pattern of which they are perceived to be a part. Episodes of teacher behavior can be compared to words in sentences: it is the sentence that gives the word meaning. And it is the paragraph that gives meaning to the sentence. If teachers or candidates are judged on the basis of checklists of discrete demonstrable skills, there is danger that the really influential aspect of teaching, that is, the meaning individual learners assign to teacher behaviors, will be overlooked. It may be that individual children assign meanings to teacher behavior that observers may either define differently or not recognize. If there are wide differences between the meanings assigned to teacher behavior episodes by observers and by pupils, the observations are unlikely to be useful for prediction or generalization. Isolated snap judgments can be made about the presence or absence of teacher behavior, but not about the meaning of teacher behavior. While the intentions of the competency-based programs seem to be to equip candidates with a "beginner's" repertoire of skills, the consequences of their programs seem to be to reduce or eliminate larger concerns of occupational socialization.

The potential risks of competency-based assessment in teacher education must be weighed against the risks of alternative approaches. One common practice is to rely on course grades. If a candidate passes all courses, including practicums, certification usually follows. In some countries a combination of courses and a state-board-type written examination is used.[11] In others, heavy reliance is placed on oral examinations, sometimes conducted by external examiners. Some institutions give more consideration to the ratings of those who supervise field work. As has already been indicated, considerable enthusiam has developed for using performance criteria.

It is likely that every approach to assessment is liable to error. Assessments that rely on course grades tend to reward candidates who are good at being students in the conventional sense. The amount and type of error in such an approach are probably related to the extent to which being good at performing the student role is compatible with being good at performing the teaching role. State-board-type examinations, such as those given by the National Nursery Examination Board in Great Britain, may make a similar error of inducting the verbally skillful when it is strong interpersonal skills that are needed. Assessments made by field supervisory personnel often err through personality conflicts between candidates and supervisors. No data have been found to demonstrate potential error in oral examinations. One possible error of this approach might be the acceptance of candidates deemed "worthy" by the examiners, or "inbreeding."

Combinations of assessment procedures (for example, performance criteria plus course grades, plus personal interviews, plus supervisor's ratings) may either help to counterbalance the errors of each ap-

proach, or they may compound the errors. But economic considerations alone may make such combinations impractical.

Assessing the outcomes of teacher education seems to be a question
of which errors we prefer to make. Inasmuch as the *meaning* of a
teacher's behavior seems to be the crux of effectiveness, the errors inherent in narrowly defined performance criteria seem to be least acceptable. Intersubjective judgments of fairly large samples of a candidate's teaching made by several staff members may minimize undesir-
able errors, but an error-free assessment strategy is not likely to be
found.

Candidates

Although there are some data concerning background characteristics of teachers in conventional public schools in the United States[12]
and in Britain,[13] I have found neither definitive nor descriptive reports
concerning characteristics of candidates for teaching in early childhood programs. Since there is no agency responsible for gathering
data on day-care and preschool personnel, an overall picture of early
childhood personnel is not available.

In 1972 Jacqueline Rosen[14] reported a study of the relationship between student teachers' effectiveness with children of different ages
and their reports of their own childhoods. Examining thirty-seven
autobiographical statements submitted during application for admission to a graduate teacher education program, the investigator looked
for characteristic themes. Relationships were sought between the
themes and the age group with which candidates' advisers rated them
as effective. Rosen's findings show that candidates who seemed most
comfortable working with children in the two- to five-year age group
had experienced "a close and supportive family life, . . . a strong sense
of love and personal security, and . . . gratification."[15] These candidates also "underplayed the academic aspects of school experience."
Candidates rated most comfortable and competent with children from
five to eight years old were more inclined to "push toward mastery,"
and to underplay affective themes. Candidates who were more comfortable with eight- to eleven-year-old students and revealed a "love of
learning" reported having been affected by teachers who were intellectually exciting and recalled the intellectual and cultural flavor of their
homes. It is not clear whether the findings imply that candidates
should be screened for their potential success with preschool children

or whether something should be done to increase the capacity of candidates in the other two groups to be comfortable with younger children.

There is a tendency to recruit candidates for teaching the young from among ethnic minority groups, but the success of this effort has not yet been reliably documented. There is also interest in attracting male candidates to teach in preschool programs. These may be facets, but as yet there does not appear to be any overall picture of candidates in early childhood teacher education. Rosen's research does underscore a common theme in early childhood education literature, namely, that personal characteristics — socioeconomic background, ethnic origin, attitudes, and beliefs — of the candidate are crucial to performance.

Staff Participants

Studies of characteristics of staff members involved with early childhood teacher education programs, like those of candidates for teaching positions, are also lacking. Inasmuch as a staff can include graduate student assistants, laboratory school teachers, on-site day-care and preschool personnel, and community college instructors, as well as conventional faculty members affiliated with teacher education, child development, and home economics programs operating in a variety of settings, a variety of characteristics could be expected.

Potential questions concerning staff characteristics are numerous. The absence of any established or accepted paradigm delineating teacher education makes it difficult even to agree on which questions are most urgent, but the framework of occupational socialization leads me to suggest a few possible ones.

Staff members, seen as agents of occupational socialization, can be thought of as helping candidates to acquire the "occupational personality" referred to by Howard Becker and J. W. Carper: "occupational identifications are internalized by the individual in the course of his entrance into the passage through a set of training institutions."[16] Two questions arise: How can staff members assist candidates in acquiring an "occupational personality"? Is such an acquisition desirable?

It would also be interesting to know to what extent and in what ways staff members serve as models for candidates. If, for example, staff members were asked to enumerate a list of "professional" attributes they wished to foster in candidates, to what extent would candidates perceive the same attributes in the staff? General impressions suggest that candidates at both the preservice and the in-service levels perceive staff members to be impractical and too far removed from the realities of day-to-day work in programs with children.

General impressions also suggest that staff members themselves suffer from low morale, and they are often cynical about the usefulness of their efforts. Teacher educators working in large institutions may perceive themselves to have low prestige and status in the eyes of their colleagues. Early childhood staffs may perceive themselves to have low status compared to colleagues in other subfields of education. The extent to which these perceptions exist and are accurate readings of colleagues' attributions is in need of verification.

Again, questions arise: Do candidates perceive the teacher education staff (at senior colleges particularly) to be as competent intellectually as their instructors of courses outside of education (for example, in psychology, biology, Western civilization)? What might be the relative standings of teacher educators and noneducation instructors in terms of the occupational socialization process?

Program Content

There appears to be little agreement on what knowledge, skills, ideas, and facts the candidates specializing in early childhood education should have. Some specialists feel that teachers need only to know how to generate lesson plans from statements of behavioral objectives; others say they need the special kind of knowledge that comes from having the same ethic and socioeconomic background as the children to be served; still others claim that what the teacher needs most is knowledge and acceptance of self.

Most programs seem to assume that candidates should have at least some knowledge of child development. Even competency-based programs tend to include "demonstrations" of knowledge of child development. Just how much knowledge constitutes "enough" is not clear; nor are there data available by which to assess the validity of the assumption. Beyond these more basic questions, it is not clear which approaches to child development — for example, Piagetian, Eriksonian, behavioristic — are considered essential, or how the knowledge of child development "works" for candidates. It seems reasonable to assume that the child development knowledge base serves to provide candidates with baselines or norm references by which to assess child behavior, with appropriate responses, and with suitable activities. Such a knowledge base frees candidates from having to apply only spe-

cifically rehearsed techniques and enables them to generate unre-
hearsed techniques from the understandings such knowledge provides.
These assumptions, again, need to be tested.

Although all teacher educators and candidates seem to agree on the
importance of field experience or practice teaching, the proportion of
time allocated to it varies. The CDA Program specifies that 50 percent
of training must be field based. Conventional teacher education programs allocate a much smaller proportion of time to actual practice in
the field.

There appears to be general agreement on the usefulness of practicums, but they also pose problems. In many communities situations
where candidates can observe "good" practices are in short supply.
Sometimes candidates complain of having to engage in teaching practices that their teacher educators reject or deplore. It is not actually
clear what candidates do learn from such experiences. Often their responses to "bad" placement can be broadly typed as excessive idealism
or excessive realism.[17] One candidate reacted to a "bad" classroom by
saying, "now I know exactly what I will never do when I'm a teacher."
This reflected a highly idealized version of future occupational performance. Excessive realism, in contrast, refers to acceptance of what
is observed in the field as the upper and outer limits of what is possible
or what must be the nature of practice. One of the functions of the
practicum supervisor, it would appear, is balancing realism with
idealism, leaving open the range of what is possible.

The truism that "practice makes perfect" is common sense. But
common sense may overlook the point that only "good" practice
makes perfect. It can be argued that candidates can and do learn from
imperfect or even "bad" field placements. Just what is learned and
how it is learned are not, however, clear.[18] If candidates can, indeed,
learn what they need to know from "bad" placements, there need be
no undue anxiety about the quality of placements, and practicums
would be more rewarding for candidates.

It would be impractical and economically unfeasible to plan to
"cover" all potentially useful knowledge and skill content. Some
choices must be made, and, to an extent, those choices are based on
tradition or habit. In view of necessary limitations, teacher educators
should perhaps try to cultivate in candidates the desire or disposition
to be continuous learners. One way to strengthen such a disposition
might be to indicate to candidates that their preservice experiences are

intended to provide a beginning set of skills, a "survival kit" to serve only until they are sufficiently settled into their occupational roles. Teacher educators seem to encounter competing pressures with respect to choice of content: tradition versus innovation in developing techniques and skills. Where tradition is followed, staffs fail to upgrade or improve conventional practices. In the latter case they risk producing maladaptive graduates. Perhaps it might be possible to introduce candidates to both conventional and innovative practices and at the same time give them insight into the nature of the competing pressures.

Time

The activities that constitute a teacher education program vary as to the total period of time in which they occur and as to the point in time, during that period, when they occur. There may also be variations as to the sequence or order in which activities occur.

Stanton Wheeler[19] suggests that a lengthy stay in a socialization setting increases "the formation of a strong cohesive culture among recruits." In academic institutions the concept of "residency" implies that candidates acquire valuable attributes from continuous and intensive contact with agents of socialization in the setting. Time spent, as a discrete variable, may not, however, be sufficient for successful socialization.[20] The frequency, intensity, and kind of contacts may be copredictors of the outcomes of the socialization process.

Some competency-based programs provide flexibility in the duration of candidacy. It is not yet known how much variation there can be in total time spent. Certainly it is possible that the acquisition of specific demonstrable skills can be accelerated, but the role of time in modifying teaching style and providing occupational identification may be more complex.

Obviously duration of candidacy affects the number of opportunities to engage in given activities. When time is limited, choices must again be made. It would be of some interest to know on what bases allocations of time are made, as well as the extent to which variations in time allocations are related to the outcomes of teacher education.

At present there is strong pressure for practicums to be offered earlier rather than later in the sequence of activities of a program. One strong argument in favor of early practicums is that they provide candidates with opportunities to "try on" the teacher role and to make an informed career choice prior to the completion of much of their required work. Another argument is that simultaneous as well as subsequent course work becomes more relevant after "trying on" the teacher role and exercising teaching techniques. There is as yet no evidence to support these arguments, and the effects of placing candidates in a "bad" field setting may be more detrimental earlier in the candidacy period than later.[21] Flexibility in timing and sequencing may be especially useful in designing programs when candidates vary as to age and life experiences.[22]

The concept of developmental stages of teacher growth has appeared in the professional literature.[23] Research suggests that concerns and developmental tasks vary as candidates progress through the activities program. It seems reasonable to hypothesize that understandings of teaching develop as experience accrues. It also seems reasonable to assume that candidates' understanding of what teaching involves would be less finely and fully differentiated earlier in their careers. Differentiation could be expected to increase when arriving at conceptions of teaching situations, attributing the causes of children's behavior, and in similar instances. The early-stage candidate is likely to have a narrow range of responses to teaching situations; the later-stage candidate is more likely to request additional information or to say "it depends."[24]

Ethos

Ethos, like social climate, may be defined as "the feeling tone which expresses something about the feelings generated by the total set of relations between staff and recruits."[25] The ethos of a socialization setting may be related to the candidates' acquisition of teaching style as well as their occupational identity.

The ethos of early childhood teacher socialization settings is likely to emphasize empathy, acceptance, and love of children; intellectual (not academic) development of candidates is underemphasized. It is not clear how an ethos is created or maintained. There may be a stereotype in our culture that those who are warm and caring are not very bright, while those who are bright are cold. This myth is strengthened by some candidates' reports that they were counseled to enter early childhood education because they were not capable of doing other college work. Such counseling seems to be related to candidates' tendencies to be preoccupied with being or becoming a person who "loves children," and thereby renounces deeper intellectual pursuits and development.

One factor that affects the ethos of a socialization setting is size. A program that is too small could yield problems of overintimacy, insufficient variety of participants at candidate and staff levels, and deficiencies in resources.

On the other hand, in larger teacher education settings the feeling tone is likely to be flat or lacking in either social or intellectual vitality. As numbers of candidates and staff members increase, the ability to create and maintain a given ethos may decrease and the need for regimentation or bureaucratization may increase. To use an analogy, the ethos bears a closer resemblance to a cafeteria than it does to a dining room, and cafeterias seem deficient both affectively and aesthetically when contrasted with dining rooms. The disadvantages of the "cafeteria"-type of atmosphere seem highlighted when contrasted with the small charismatic institutions that have had a special and historic role in early childhood education.[26] Research on the role of ethos in the socialization process could be revealing.

Location and Setting

There are many variables in this class. One that is of special interest is the extent to which the activities and experiences provided in a teacher education setting can be generalized when the candidate is employed. In laboratory or demonstration settings candidates may be surrounded by talent, resources, and congenial peers. This is not often duplicated in the work situation. Is the gradient of generalization from the preservice to the in-service setting too steep? What provisions should be made for smooth transition? To what extent should the activities of a teacher education program be located away from a campus?

Regulation

Early childhood teacher education programs are affected by the regulations of a variety of agencies: state social welfare and education departments, federal guidelines, and intramural procedures. Regulations can impinge on the content of programs and on the way a candidate's time is allocated.

There have been informal reports of candidates threatening to sue educational institutions when denied certification. These reports are worth investigating since such threats serve to reduce emphasis on the less observable segments of the occupation (such as teaching style and occupational identity) and increase emphasis on the "demonstrable skills" of teaching, a tendency already observable.

A sizable body of data on the teaching of young children has been developed during the last decade, but there has been little empirical work on teacher education. Perhaps the next decade will witness the development of a professional organization that will coordinate research efforts, gather information, and stimulate investigation in an attempt to answer some of the questions that it was only possible to pose here.

Notes

1. This description of training for nursery teachers is attributed to Jessie Stanton in Evelyn Beyer, *Teaching Young Children* (New York: Pegasus, 1968), 78.

2. Orville G. Brim, Jr., "Socialization through the Life Cycle," in Orville G. Brim, Jr., and Stanton Wheeler, *Socialization after Childhood: Two Essays* (New York: John Wiley & Sons, 1966). 1–49.

3. W. E. Moore, *The Professions: Roles and Rules* (New York: Russell Sage Foundation, 1970), 71.

4. Edward Zigler, "A New Child Care Profession: The Child Development Associate," *Young Children* 27 (December 1971): 71–74.

5. Evelyn Weber, "The Function of Early Childhood Education," *Young Children* 28 (June 1973): 265–274; Bernard Spodek, "Early Childhood Education and Teacher Education: A Search for Consistency," *Young Children* 30 (March 1975): 168–173. See also *Preschool Education, A Handbook for the Training of Early Childhood Educators*, ed. Ralph W. Colvin and Esther M. Zaffiro (New York: Springer Publishing Co., 1974), 113–198.

6. *Child Development Associate Training Guide* (Washington, D.C.: Office of Child Development, U. S. Department of Health, Education, and Welfare, No. 73-1065, April 1973); Jenny W. Klein and C. Ray Williams, "The Development of the Child Development Associate (CDA) Program," *Young Children* 28 (February 1973): 139–145.

7. Klein and Williams, "The Development of the Child Development Associate Program," 142.

8. *Ibid.*, 142–143.

9. E. Kuno Beller, "Adult-Child Interaction and Personalized Day Care," in *Day Care: Resources for Decisions*, ed. Edith Grotberg (Washington, D.C.: Office of Economic Opportunity, 1970), 229–264.

10. J. M. Merrow, *Politics of Competence: A Review of Competency-Based Teacher Education* (Washington, D.C.: National Institute of Education, U. S. Department of Health, Education, and Welfare, 1975).

11. National Nursery Examination Board, *Regulations and Syllabus for the Examination of the National Nursery Examination Board* (London: National Nursery Examination Board, 1974).

12. Richard L. Turner, "An Overview of Research in Teacher Education," in *Teacher Education*, Seventy-fourth Yearbook of the National Society for the Study of Education, Part II, ed. Kevin Ryan (Chicago: University of Chicago Press, 1975), 87–110.

13. Donald E. Lomax, "A Review of British Research in Teacher Education," *Review of Educational Research* 42 (Summer 1972): 289–326.

14. Jacqueline L. Rosen, "Matching Teachers with Children," *School Review* 80 (May 1972): 409–431.

15. *Ibid.*, 415.

16. Howard S. Becker and J. W. Carper, "The Development of Identification with an Occupation," *American Journal of Sociology* 61 (January 1956): 289–298.

17. See Lilian G. Katz, "Issues and Problems in Teacher Education," in *Teacher Education*, ed. Bernard Spodek (Washington, D.C.: National Association for the Education of Young Children, 1974), 55–66.

18. *Ibid.*

19. Stanton Wheeler, "The Structure of Formally Organized Socialization Settings," in Brim, *Socialization after Childhood*, 51–107.

20. A. B. Campbell, "The Influence of Contact, Compatability, Similarity, Esteem and Control on Student Teacher Modeling of Cooperating Teacher Style of Program Planning," unpublished dissertation, University of Illinois, Urbana-Champaign, 1975.

21. See Katz, "Issues and Problems in Teacher Education," and Constance A. Shorter, "Field Experiences of Sophomore Students in Two Preservice Teacher Education Programs," unpublished dissertation, University of Illinois, Urbana-Champaign, 1975.

22. Shorter, "Field Experiences of Sophomore Students."

23. Frances F. Fuller and Oliver Bown, "Becoming a Teacher," in *Teacher Education*, ed. Ryan, 25–52.

24. See Ann M. Bussis and Edward A. Chittenden, *Analysis of an Approach to Open Education: Interim Report* (Princeton, N.J.: Educational Testing Service, 1970).

25. Wheeler, "Structure of Formally Organized Socialization Settings."

26. Katz, "Issues and Problems in Teacher Education."